UNDERSTANDING
LEE SMITH

UNDERSTANDING CONTEMPORARY AMERICAN LITERATURE
Matthew J. Bruccoli, Founding Editor
Linda Wagner-Martin, Series Editor

UNDERSTANDING

LEE SMITH

Danielle N. Johnson

The University of South Carolina Press

© 2018 University of South Carolina

Published by the University of South Carolina Press
Columbia, South Carolina 29208

www.sc.edu/uscpress

Manufactured in the United States of America

27 26 25 24 23 22 21 20 19 18
10 9 8 7 6 5 4 3 2 1

Library of Congress Cataloging-in-Publication Data
can be found at http://catalog.loc.gov/.

ISBN 978-1-61117-880-7 (cloth)
ISBN 978-1-61117-881-4 (ebook)

This book was printed on recycled paper with
30 percent postconsumer waste content.

To Bryce, Phineas, and Reid

CONTENTS

SERIES EDITOR'S PREFACE

The Understanding Contemporary American Literature series was founded by the estimable Matthew J. Bruccoli (1931–2008), who envisioned these volumes as guides or companions for students as well as good nonacademic readers, a legacy that will continue as new volumes are developed to fill in gaps among the nearly one hundred series volumes published to date and to embrace a host of new writers only now making their marks on our literature.

As Professor Bruccoli explained in his preface to the volumes he edited, because much influential contemporary literature makes special demands, "the word *understanding* in the titles was chosen deliberately. Many willing readers lack an adequate understanding of how contemporary literature works; that is, of what the author is attempting to express and the means by which it is conveyed." Aimed at fostering this understanding of good literature and good writers, the criticism and analysis in the series provide instruction in how to read certain contemporary writers—explicating their material, language, structures, themes, and perspectives—and facilitate a more profitable experience of the works under discussion.

In the twenty-first century Professor Bruccoli's prescience gives us an avenue to publish expert critiques of significant contemporary American writing. The series continues to map the literary landscape and to provide both instruction and enjoyment. Future volumes will seek to introduce new voices alongside canonized favorites, to chronicle the changing literature of our times, and to remain, as Professor Bruccoli conceived, contemporary in the best sense of the word.

Linda Wagner-Martin, Series Editor

ACKNOWLEDGMENTS

I began to study Lee Smith at the University of North Carolina at Chapel Hill, and I am grateful to many people there. Professors Minrose Gwin, Maria DeGuzman, Fred Hobson, Bland Simpson, Linda Wagner-Martin, Ruth Salvaggio, Susan Irons, Peter Filene, and the late Darryl Gless have been especially generous. Lauren Cameron and Christy Webb Clemons are brilliant colleagues and friends. I thank Algonquin Books of Chapel Hill, which supported this book by providing me an advance copy of Smith's *Dimestore* (2016). I also enthusiastically thank Lee Smith, who has been uncommonly accessible and kind throughout this project.

Jenny Jackson introduced me to Smith's work—as well as to that of other essential writers—years before I might otherwise have discovered it. With help from Sara Weishampel and Krystal Lancaster, she also led me to believe that I could write a book. My parents, Ron and Annette Hartman, encouraged my early and consuming interest in reading and writing and gave me space to do both. I also thank David and Kelsey Hartman, Holli and Dan Herr, Ashley and Ryan Swartz, Allison Hartman, Lindsay and Brad Tripp, Teresa Johnson, and Emily Meeks. I'm glad to do it all alongside Bryce.

CHAPTER 1

Understanding Lee Smith

In the five decades since the release of her first novel, *The Last Day the Dog-bushes Bloomed* (1968), Lee Smith has published broadly and prolifically. She has matched the commercial success of works such as *The Last Girls* (2002), which was chosen for the *Good Morning America* Book Club and became a *New York Times* bestseller, with academic and critical respect garnered by such novels as *Oral History* (1983), *Fair and Tender Ladies* (1988), and *On Agate Hill* (2006). Among other honors, Smith has received the O. Henry Award, the Sir Walter Raleigh Award, the Robert Penn Warren Prize for Fiction, and the Reader's Digest Award. A half-dozen of her novels and stories have been adapted for the stage by the actress Barbara Bates Smith, and *Good Ol' Girls,* an off-Broadway musical based on her stories and those of the writer Jill McCorkle, has been produced in many locations since its 2010 Manhattan premiere. Despite her varied and prolific output, there are certain areas of focus that have defined Smith's writing life. She has consistently returned to issues of female subjectivity and the value of self-expression, working through the intersections of women's lives with literacy, artistry, religion, history, and love. She approaches these weighty subjects with generosity and humor.

In nearly all her published writing, Smith blurs the distinction between art and self-expression, particularly for female characters. Her novels and stories often highlight talented, but unheralded, small-town people, most of whom would not call themselves artists. From self-employed seamstresses making slipcovers to front-porch musicians playing fiddles, Smith creates characters whose humble artistry may belie its obscurity. Art in much of Smith's fiction is most valuable to its creator, whose considered self-expression it represents. She underscores the importance of identity by often writing in the first-person voices of rural women, further challenging through her narration what the critic Paul Lauter has called "special privilege," or, "the special languages that specially-trained critics share with specially-cultivated poets" (140). Such specialized languages, Lauter argues, exist mostly to defend the perceived value of both selected works of art and the criticism that addresses them. By her rejection of formal language in favor of colloquial, and of official histories for subjective ones, Smith upends traditional measures of artistic value. And by focusing on the lives of storytellers and other, perhaps unrecognized, artists, Smith asserts the historical significance of widely unheard narratives. Consistently, Smith champions female subjectivity at nearly any cost.

Smith's challenges to traditional conceptions of art and personal success are both class-conscious and gender-based. Though her rural narrators occasionally come from or into money, they rarely grow wealthy from the practice of their crafts. Instead, following their passions often leads Smith's characters away from financial security. Ivy Rowe, for instance, the hero of Smith's 1988 *Fair and Tender Ladies,* can neither leave her hometown to pursue an education—she becomes pregnant, gives birth, and will not abandon her child—or to marry her rich, reckless suitor, Franklin Ransom, whom she does not love. Though either course might have made Ivy's life a more financially comfortable one, she rejects both and instead remains near her rural home, Sugar Fork, where her writing goes unnoticed and her choices mostly are her own. That Ivy's path is her own does not mean that it is easy: her poverty and other factors continually make it difficult for her to negotiate her identity not only as an artist but also as a mother, a daughter, and a wife. She is typical, in this way, of other women in Smith's writing. The forces that stand in the way of their aims and instincts often are well meaning; relatives of female artists, for instance, urge adherence to tradition or to social convention. Florrie, an eccentric baker in the short story "Cakewalk," is a predecessor of Ivy in this regard. Her prim sister, Stella, "wouldn't be caught dead" in Florrie's colorful outfits and chastises Florrie for flouting their mother's rules of decorum (*Cakewalk* 226).

Smith's emphasis on literacy and creativity is expressed through the format of her fiction as well as through its content. By using diaries and oral narratives to structure her novels she reaffirms the value of personal, and even private, storytelling. The critic Lillian Robinson refers to real-life counterparts of the fictional Ivy Rowe when she describes how, in recent years, more—and more diverse—women began to eke out recognition as "good" writers. "Feminist scholarship," she claims, "has also pushed back the boundaries of literature in other directions, considering a wide range of forms and styles in which women's writing—especially that of women who did not perceive themselves as writers—appears. In this way, women's letters, diaries, journals, autobiographies, oral histories, and private poetry have come under critical scrutiny as evidence of women's consciousness *and expression*" (124). Robinson highlights here the importance of writing as a means of expression, so central to Ivy Rowe's life-long impulse to write.

In her fiction Smith expands the boundaries of noteworthy expression to include the artistry of women with talents besides writing. Florrie, for instance, achieves expression through her cakes; Candy Snipes, of 1985's *Family Linen,* is a small-town beautician. Both women are able to live from the profits of their artistry, though neither is at all wealthy; they stand out as particularly fulfilled characters in Smith's oeuvre because they make a living doing what they love. Katie Cocker of *The Devil's Dream* (1992) is a famous country-music singer and songwriter and the rare Smith character to gain both fortune and fulfill-ment from her artistry. Despite her relatively privileged position, Katie is not an oversimplified character. She battles addiction, endures loss, and admits to compromising her artistic vision during periods of her career.

It would be an exaggeration to say that Smith "celebrates" all sorts of wom-en's artistry, but her fiction recognizes and respects the skill and passion that her female characters invest in varied pursuits. Smith also recognizes creative output as important for self-knowledge and survival. In her 1990 story "Bob, a Dog" newly divorced Cheryl gains a feeling of control over her life as a single mother by sewing slipcovers. Cheryl's are domestic artifacts so humble that they soak up children's spills and swaddle television-watching adults, but they enable her to earn a living and connect her to her relatively supportive social community. In her fiction and her life Smith challenges the primacy of art that is perceived as sophisticated. "It's like the knitting of a sweater, the making of the quilt, and that kind of thing," Smith told Pat Arnow in a 1989 interview. "That something is art even though it's not perceived as public art. It's the dif-ference between monumental sculpture and needlepoint" (Tate 63).

Women in Smith's early novels who are not confident in their abilities, who find themselves without social position or talent, usually are doomed: their communities are inclined to push them over the edge rather than to sup-port them. This trend reached its apex in Smith's *Black Mountain Breakdown* (1980). In that work Crystal Spangler is so defined by others and so paralyzed by choices that she retreats into a catatonic state; she becomes a beautiful shell. Crystal is a good teacher and a good writer, but she does not believe enough in either talent to forge a sense of self. Smith underscores Crystal's exteriority by comparing her to mirrors and crystals. She is the literary personification of a contemporary essay by the scholars Sandra M. Gilbert and Susan Gubar, "Infec-tion in the Sentence," first published in 1979. They write: "Learning to become a beautiful object, the girl learns anxiety about—perhaps even loathing of

—her own flesh. Peering obsessively into the real as well as metaphorical looking glasses that surround her, she desires literally to 'reduce' her own body" (27). For Crystal, this desire literally paralyzes her.

As Smith's career progressed, however, she began to believe in better outcomes for the women in her narratives. As Nancy Parrish put it, "Her early stories describe girls and young women who have been literally or figuratively silenced, limited, or raped. Her later novels reveal women who have resisted cultural restraints, found their own voices, and succeeded at unique life goals that oppose conventional expectations" (*Lee Smith* 166). Katie Cocker often is cited as a woman who typifies a hero of Smith's fiction from the mid-1980s forward. Katie tries on different identities as a singer determined by her family, her producers, and her boyfriends, but ultimately she settles into lyrics and music that are uniquely hers. Mary Copeland of *The Christmas Letters* (1996) and Molly Petree of *On Agate Hill* (2006) are similarly positioned, suggesting the staying power of Smith's shift in perspective.

As she highlights female artistry and identity in settings from the early nineteenth century to the present, Smith necessarily questions accepted historical narratives. Reassessing the roles of women in history requires that Smith reevaluate history itself. As Gilbert and Gubar have written, "If [we ask] where does a woman writer 'fit in' to the overwhelmingly and essentially male literary history [Harold] Bloom describes?—we have to answer that a woman writer does not 'fit in.' At first glance, indeed, she seems to be anomalous, indefinable, alienated, a freakish outsider" (23). Smith redefines history in her fiction by examining her outsiders' plights and also by creating some historical spaces in which they need not be outsiders. In *On Agate Hill,* for instance, Smith undermines Civil War tropes through the writing of her character Molly Petree, an antebellum orphan whose diary grounds the novel. Molly discovers that her ladylike mother's former lover, Simon, was born to a poor blacksmith. Though Simon seems to be a commanding, wealthy Southern gentleman, he is revealed to have made his fortune in Brazil after the war. Simon's story is surprising to Molly and, probably, to many of Smith's readers. By mining relatively obscure historical records—the expatriated *Confederados,* in this case—Smith suggests the breadth of history that underlies what is most often recorded and taught.

In emphasizing this breadth Smith often examines the past in rural locales and domestic settings, elevating the everyday to the realm of history. In addition to her unconventional coverage of the Civil War in *On Agate Hill,* Smith describes, in that same novel, learning and teaching in the antebellum period. As a teenager, Molly Petree attends an expensive religiously affiliated girls' school in Eastern Virginia and goes on, as a young woman, to instruct relatively poor mountain children of all ages in a one-room schoolhouse. Using historical research as a basis for her narrative, Smith gives the postbellum home front attention often reserved for tales of the battlefield or courtroom. Similarly, in *The Devil's Dream,* Smith's exploration of country music, the author dwells largely in the hollers and hills of Western Virginia, moving the novel to Nashville only in its late narrative. By tracing the origins of her subject to the rural mountains Smith issues a gentle reminder that country music did not begin with an eruption of rhinestones and cowboy hats. She instead situates the origins of the genre at the intersection of religion and good-time music, telling stories along the way of conflicted mountain families.

In many respects Smith as a writer participates in the reshaping of cultural memory as she highlights unfamiliar artists. She simultaneously encourages skepticism about institutional histories. As explained by Marianne Hirsch and Valerie Smith, cultural memory is "the juncture where the individual and the social come together, where the person is called upon to illustrate the social formation in its heterogeneity and complexity" (Hirsch and Smith 7). Hirsch and Smith explain how individual narratives are capable of presenting "a challenge and a countermemory to official hegemonic history" (7). Smith's novels and stories are full of countermemories, from Alice Petree's love for the son of her wealthy family's blacksmith in *On Agate Hill* to a contemporary's impression of Zelda Fitzgerald in *Guests on Earth* (2013). However, Smith does not simply create her own alternate histories. Instead, she encourages her readers to share their own experiences, to shape history through their own stories. In her fiction Smith does this through her extensive use of vernacular first-person voice.

Smith's approach to religion is similar; she depicts faith positively when it is personalized but scrutinizes the patriarchal control it often is marshaled to support. Ivy Rowe, especially, states clearly her inability to accept the Christian doctrine that guides most people in her mountain community. Though Ivy feels a spiritual connection to the physical elements around her—ice crystals, spring breezes, budding branches—she feels little emotional connection to religious services. She cannot stomach the hypocrisy of many of the Christians she encounters. The critic Conrad Ostwalt persuasively argues that, in *Fair and Tender Ladies* and elsewhere, Smith relies on images to convey a "dual religious consciousness" in her writing. The first, he says, "appears in the form of traditional religions that attempt to transcend the mountain peaks and valley floors," while the second "is characterized by an elemental, supernatural power bound up by nature and the mountains themselves" (98). Smith consistently is more sympathetic to an "elemental" spirituality, although she occasionally features a protagonist who finds a way for herself as a Christian. In *Saving Grace* (1995) particularly, the victim of a philandering evangelical father eventually finds comfort and salvation in Christianity as practiced by her gentle mother.

Though Grace is scarred by her father and later by her marriage to the kind but ascetic minister Travis Word, she seeks a different, more nurturing approach to Christianity instead of abandoning it entirely. By including relatively unconventional sources of spiritual inspiration and religious practice in her fiction, Smith underscores her regard for individual expression and the need for opposition to forces that seek to limit it.

Smith's own writing life began during her girlhood in Grundy, Virginia, a small mountain community in the southwestern corner of the state. "When I was a child," she writes in *Dimestore* (2016), "books brought my deepest pleasure, my greatest excitement. Reading, I often felt exactly the way I did during summer thunderstorms: I just had to run out of the house and up the mountain into the very storm to whirl in the thunder and rain" (101). Smith soon began writing, too, and drafted her first, unpublished novel in Grundy at the age of eight. In *Jane Russell and Adlai Stevenson Go West in a Covered Wagon*, the title characters eventually marry and convert to Mormonism. In an interview with Peter Guralnick included in *Conversations with Lee Smith* (2001), Smith claimed that the handwritten story is closely related to her later fiction. Motifs of "religion and flight, staying in one place or not staying, [and] containment," she notes, are all there on her mother's blue stationary (Tate 143). Smith also practiced her newswriting in Grundy, circulating with a friend a problematic hand-copied newsletter they called the *Small Review*. "I got in lots of trouble for my editorials," Smith writes in *Dimestore*, "such as 'George McGuire Is Too Grumpy,' or my opinion that 'Mrs. Ruth Boyd is a mean music teacher" (*Dimestore* 17).

The only child of mature parents, Smith was encouraged to write from childhood by her father in particular. Ernest Smith owned and operated a general store downtown, which brought his daughter into frequent contact with her community. His extended family also lived nearby, so Smith spent her childhood with houses full of cousins, aunts, and uncles. Despite his family's roots in Grundy—at the time of Lee Smith's birth, Ernest Smith's ancestors had lived in Grundy for at least four generations—Ernest Smith was somewhat set apart. After brief periods away to fight in World War II and play football for the College of William and Mary, Ernest Smith returned with "notions," reciting poetry around town and developing ideas for his Ben Franklin store (Tate 53). One of Ernest's innovations was a backyard "writing house" for his daughter. "I'd go out there and write," Smith recalls, "and he'd pay me a nickel if I'd write a story" (Tate 154). Smith's father also was responsible for sending her to St. Catherine's, a girls' boarding school in Richmond that none of Smith's Grundy peers attended. "My dad was literally trying to propel me outside of [the mountains]," Smith has said; "if he hadn't done this I don't know how I could have done any of the things I have" (Tate 55).

While Ernest Smith encouraged his daughter's creativity, his unique mind-set occasionally caused his daughter difficulty. "My father was overworked and had a nervous breakdown," Smith says in an interview with Virginia Smith (no relation); "once when I was a girl, both my mother and my father were in separate psychiatric hospitals at the same time" (Tate 72). When one or both of her parents had an episode, Smith spent weeks in the mountains with her cousins, temporarily becoming part of multichild households though she had no siblings. The mental illness in Smith's family inspired characters and incidents in her fiction, even as it made her fearful of the effect a writing career might have on her own sanity. "There is something scary," she told Virginia Smith, "about deciding to become a writer or painter, because you are not within comfortable boundaries" (Tate 72). Fortunately, her career has had a supportive, rather than a destructive, effect on Smith. "Writing helps her work through real-life trauma," Jeanne McDonald notes; "it's her personal brand of therapy, the way she deals with whatever emotional ups and downs she inherited from her beloved manic-depressive parents" (Tate 186).

While her father came from a long line of mountaineers, her mother Virginia—called Gig—hailed from Virginia's coastal Eastern Shore. Gig Smith taught home economics at the local school, and her studied femininity was both fascinating to and challenging for her daughter. "Despite all my own inclinations" Smith writes in "Lady Lessons," a chapter of *Dimestore*, "my mother kept at it, trying her best, raising me to be a lady" (57). Gig Smith's attempts included trips away from Grundy to visit her relatively refined family members, whom she hoped would be good influences on her tomboy daughter. Despite Smith's resistance to her mother's efforts, she credits her mother, too, with her development as a writer. "When I was little," she writes, "[Gig] read aloud to me constantly; I believe it is for this reason that I came to love reading so much, for I always heard her voice in my head as I read the words on the page" (*Sitting on the Courthouse Bench* 26). Gig Smith's experience as a Grundy transplant also informed her daughter's perspective. In a 1993 interview with Claudia Lowenstein, Smith recalls how her "mother was considered an outsider though she lived in the mountain community for sixty years" (Tate 112). Access to her mother's outlook allowed Smith to see Grundy as both insider and outsider, as did her family's relatively privileged social position. Though Smith has downplayed class divisions as being much of an influence in Grundy, she acknowledges that separation existed between children reared in town and those born in the nearby mountain hollers. "Our fortunes didn't depend on whether the mines were working or not," Smith recalls, "the unions were striking, and so on. Our fathers just didn't get killed right and left, or lose their arms" (Tate 53). Smith stayed with cousins in company towns, but she also was crowned Miss Grundy High and eventually educated at St. Catherine's: she was of Grundy, yet separate.

Though specific incidents and persons from Smith's girlhood appear in her fiction, Grundy's influence is most visible in the orality of Smith's writing. "I grew up in a family of world-class talkers," Smith told Charline McCord. "They were wonderful talkers and storytellers. . . . I really did grow up on stories" (Tate 153). Smith's frequent decision to write first-person narratives for her characters reflects her emphasis on the oral, as does her involvement in an oral history of Grundy, written by local high school students and compiled and edited by Smith. Composed mostly of interviews, *Sitting on the Courthouse Bench: An Oral History of Grundy, Virginia* (2000) eschews conventional, formal artistry for the spoken words of mostly elderly town residents. Smith includes her own family's history in the introduction to the volume. Though her piece is more obviously crafted than others in the history, she reveals similarly small details of Grundy life. She recalls, for instance, "the yellow-tiled cafeteria where I surreptitiously picked up all the Peppermint Patty wrappers ever touched by the boy I had a crush on" (25). The oral history also includes photographs of Grundy, as well as a "primer" on how to conduct an oral history for beginners.

Smith continued to write during her education at St. Catherine's and secured her first publishing contract as an undergraduate at Hollins College in Roanoke, Virginia. Initially, she kept her writing a secret. "I'd sort of hidden it because I was at St. Catherine's," she said in 1990 interview. "My father had sent me off to St. Catherine's to turn me into a lady, and it wasn't okay to be that way" (Tate 81). At Hollins, however, Smith's writing took center stage as she studied under the writer and publisher Louis Rubin with a group of talented peers, several of whom would go on to successful literary careers of their own. In her study *Lee Smith, Annie Dillard, and the Hollins Group: A Genesis of Writers,* Nancy C. Parrish describes the campus dynamic that encouraged the development of strong female voices. Smith, she writes, "experienced a sisterly community that promised to be an enduring and dependable support system" (*Lee Smith* 202). "I was among a group of girls . . . who were pretty much just like I was," Smith told Irv Broughton. "We were just all on fire with reading and writing" (Tate 81). Although Smith grew as a writer at Hollins, she did not have a conventionally successful college career. Her grades were middling in many courses, and Smith was even expelled for a semester after staying out all night during a semester in France. "I was just writing all the time, and I was excited about everything, and I somehow just couldn't seem to notice the rules" (Tate 81). Smith spent a semester working for a Richmond newspaper before she could gain readmission. "I don't know how I graduated," she has said. "I didn't try to do anything [outside of writing]. . . . I was just literally crazed with the stuff I was interested in" (Tate 81).

Smith left Hollins with the same determination to write and began a career in fiction that initially was marked by measured critical praise and modest book sales. Her first move was to revise *The Last Day the Dogbushes Bloomed*, the novel she had begun at Hollins, for publication; it was issued as a Harper & Row hardback in 1968 and republished in 1994 by Louisiana State University Press. In a *Chicago Tribune* review the influential critic Fanny Butcher wrote that the novel displayed Smith's "real gift for writing" and "great potential as a novelist." Butcher also noted, however, that she had "grave doubts" that *The Last Day the Dogbushes Bloomed* would become "one of the classics of childhood." Though Smith closely followed that publication with the novels *Something in the Wind* (1971) and *Fancy Strut* (1973), it was nearly ten years before she published her fourth book. In part, the gap between publications was because Smith's first three novels had not sold well. "All three books lost money for the company," Smith told Dorothy Combs Hill, "so when I wrote *Black Mountain Breakdown*, Harper & Row wouldn't publish it" (Tate 25). By the time she found Liz Darhansoff, a new agent who led her to the Putnam editor Faith Sale, Smith had "already applied to go back to school in special education at UNC and do something else entirely" (Tate 25).

Smith also was not writing as much because of the different directions that her family and professional life were taking. After her 1967 marriage to the poet James Seay, Smith initially worked as a writer for the *Tuscaloosa News* in Alabama and then as an English teacher at Harpeth Hall School in Nashville; she gave birth to two sons, Page and Joshua, in the meantime. "It's hard to keep [writing] when no one's publishing or taking it seriously," Smith told Hill, "and meanwhile you're neglecting your kids, or your house or whatever it is that you give up" (Tate 25). "The result," Hill writes, "was a seven-year drought, a hiatus between 'two writing careers' during which no Lee Smith novel appeared." Still, Smith did not by any means abandon writing. She won awards for some of her short fiction published during those years, such as a 1979 O. Henry Award for her story, "Mrs. Darcy Meets the Blue-Eyed Stranger at the Beach." When Smith reemerged with *Black Mountain Breakdown*, which was followed closely by *Family Linen* and *Oral History*, her fiction was much more reflective of her Appalachian roots. "During the early eighties, the mountains where I came from began to change rapidly," Smith explains in *Dimestore*. "That's when I began to tape my relatives and elderly mountain friends, collecting the old stories,

songs, and histories in earnest, with the aim of preserving the type of speech
—Appalachian English—and the ways of life of a bygone era" (175).

Smith's recognition of the narrative possibilities her homeland offered
reflected a broader twentieth-century movement to reshape perceptions of
Appalachia. As early as the 1930s "poets and fiction writers native to the mountain region began to render the experiences of ordinary Appalachian people
realistically, honestly, and sympathetically" (Miller, Hatfield, and Norman
xi). The writers' attention to realism was, at least in part, a reaction against
persistent characterizations of the region as "hillbilly," a post–Civil War stereotype that remains today. By the time Smith began writing about Appalachia,
redemptive writerly efforts by James Still and Harriette Arnow had begun to
yield results. In the 1970s "a modern-day 'handing down' of cultural knowledge
from one generation to another [took] place as a modern Appalachian sense
of *identity*, at once old and new, burst across the mountain ranges. From this
decade of creative foment came a remarkable Appalachian literary and cultural renaissance" (Miller, Hatfield, and Norman xii). The cultural knowledge
Smith mined is apparent in her fiction: storytelling, musicality, Pentecostalism,
handiwork, and specific domestic traditions all are inclusions that tie Smith to
Appalachia.

Smith's position as a Southern writer, too, has been shaped by the eventful
decades during which she emerged as a writer. As Fred Hobson has observed,
conceptions of what constituted "the South" began to change rapidly at
the same time that Smith was beginning to publish fiction. "The reality—and,
even more, the mythology—of the poor, failed, defeated, backward-looking
South," he writes, "has long since been replaced by the mythology of what in
the 1970's came to be called the Sun Belt" (Hobson 4). Smith published *Something in the Wind* (1971) and *Fancy Strut* (1973)—novels mostly set in North
Carolina and Alabama, respectively, rather than in Smith's mountains—just as,
Hobson points out, the age of air-conditioning and *Southern Living* emerged.
Clearly conscious of changing modalities in the South, Smith features a prim
racist newspaper heiress in *Fancy Strut*, setting her in opposition to members of
the town's younger, mostly middle-class population, people whom the heiress
considers hopelessly vulgar. Smith does not valorize the old guard or the new,
however; each group receives the most satirical treatment of her career.

The 1968 publication of *The Last Day the Dogbushes Bloomed* also
coincided with the height of the Civil Rights movement. Smith directly and
indirectly references the movement in her first three novels. The historian Joel
Williamson has described the intellectual climate at universities in the 1960s:
"It was as if [C. Vann Woodward's *The Strange Career of Jim Crow* (1955)],
along with the Civil Rights movement itself, blasted to smithereens a dam and

allowed pent-up scholarly concerns to pour out and flood the lands below" (17). Hollins, the private southern women's college that Smith attended, was not immune to the conversation. As Parrish writes, at Hollins, "Anne Goodwyn Jones wrote feature columns in the newspaper about race relations and student issues, and other writers such as Cindy Hardwick and Nancy Beckham wrote subsequent extensions and explorations of those arguments" (*Lee Smith* 110). Smith, too, was clearly paying attention to the conversation. Among her most classifiably Southern works, the novels *The Last Day the Dogbushes Bloomed, Something in the Wind,* and *Fancy Strut* each include African American characters, many of whom act to oppose racial discrimination. These acts are subtle in some cases—Frank, the family landscaper in *The Last Day the Dogbushes Bloomed,* refuses to speak to his white employers, relishing small acts of subversion—and more pointed in others. In *Fancy Strut,* for instance, members of the local college's Afro-American Society attempt to sue the local sheriff for discrimination. Though their cause is noble, the society's motivations are not. One rich student agrees to the lawsuit because he does not like sharing dormitory bathrooms, while his ringleader friend is desperate for publicity. Refusing to idealize characters of either race, Smith consistently provides a deceptively complex take on southern race relations.

When Smith began writing novels and stories set in Appalachia, however, African American characters largely disappeared from her fiction. These conspicuous absences, which, together, span decades, separate Smith's fiction from that of many other contemporary Southern writers. Mostly, Smith explains, she left out African American characters because of the real lack of racial diversity that she saw in the Appalachia of her childhood. "There were no black people in the county where I grew up," she has said; "I was never aware of them" (Tate 74). Though realistic, Smith's explanation remains problematic for some critics. Jocelyn Hazelwood Donlon, for instance, argues that Smith is an example of an author who uses "storytelling voices which implicitly position racial audiences as primary and secondary (32). It also is true that, despite the lack of an African American population in Grundy, men and women of color have and do call Appalachia home. The so-called Affrilachian Poets, for instance, formed a writers' group in Lexington, Kentucky, in the early 1990s. According to the critic Theresa L. Burriss, the literary emphases of the Affrilachians resemble Smith's. "A focus on ancestors, common people, and their role in shaping identity pervades their writing," she notes (316). Though Smith herself did not come in contact with African Americans in her corner of Appalachia, they, too, are part of her region's story.

None of this is to say, however, that Smith ignores racial differences in her writing. Rather she mostly has written outside of the black-white binary that has sometimes characterized Southern literature, frequently featuring characters of ambiguous, Native American, or mixed races. Katerina Prajznerová has written a study of Cherokee elements in four of Smith's novels, highlighting the way Appalachian storytelling and healing traditions, among other rituals, can be attributed to Cherokee influence. "Traditional Cherokee culture and Smith's Appalachian novels," she argues, "share a belief that nature is a living spiritual force and that stories are organic cultural sources within nature" (40). Smith also has included racially distinct characters in her narratives, marking them as different without specifying their origins. The most prominent of these characters are Ora Mae and Vashti Cantrell of *Oral History,* both of whom "look like they might be part Indian," according to characters in the novel (86). In a 2001 interview with Prajznerová, Smith confirmed her intention that Vashti and Ora Mae be read as Native Americans. "I've always been really fascinated with . . . this sense of the other. . . . I was just always so curious bout Melungeons or about Indians or about people that lived way, way up in the hills" (100). The former group that Smith mentions, Melungeons, also figure prominently in *The Devil's Dream,* where the family patriarch is descended from "a race of people which nobody knows where they came from, with real pale light eyes, and dark skin, and frizzy hair like sheep's wool" (57). Through her inclusion of racially ambiguous characters, Smith signals her willingness to engage issues of racism and difference outside of the black-white binary.

Smith has been compared to her contemporaries writing fiction set in Appalachia, particularly Bobbie Ann Mason, and also to writers firmly entrenched in the South, many of whom came before her. Comparisons to Mason largely stem from the writers' somewhat similar subject matter, which includes unpretentious men and women in modest homes thinking about television shows, diets, and romantic relationships. Smith, however, graciously disputes comparisons much as she does classifications. "In terms of themes, we pretty much deal with a lot of the same thing," she acknowledged of Mason. "Her prose style though is so much more controlled, it's just beautifully controlled" (Tate 14). The trouble of assigning a label to Smith's work is evident in even a brief look at the other writers to whom Smith has been compared. H. H. Campbell, for instance, ties Smith to the Brontë sisters, noting areas in which Smith's plotting and naming of characters seem to have been influenced by the British writers. Hobson, in contrast, draws a more intuitive link between Smith and William Faulkner, a comparison echoed by Margaret D. Bauer in the introduction to her 2005 study *William Faulkner's Legacy.* Bauer cites "numerous echoes of [Faulknerian] techniques, issues, and character types" in *Oral History,* particularly, but she also suggests ways in which reading Smith changes or challenges interpretations of Faulkner. "Smith's reincarnation of Faulkner's Quentin prototype in the character of Richard Burlage," she argues, "illuminates how great a role these would-be knights actually play in the oppression of rather than rescuing of southern ladies" (8). Smith has been linked, too, to Eudora Welty and Flannery O'Connor. She has for years mentored the writer Jill McCorkle. At her most slyly subversive, her tales of the southern upper-middle class remind the reader of Ellen Gilchrist's work.

As Smith evolved from a young woman writing fiction in between part-time jobs and family commitments to an established author and full-time professor, new influences began to shape her fiction. One of the most positive of these influences was her work teaching and mentoring other writers. From the class-rooms of renowned universities to the nonprofit Hindman Settlement School in Kentucky, Smith empowered artists from varied educational backgrounds. She credits her work at the Settlement School, where she began teaching in 1992 after receiving a Lila Wallace–Readers' Digest Writers' Award, with renewing her "thrill, the lightning storm," of writing. Smith's adult students there wrote poetry about their children and relationships, essays about illiteracy and self-reliance, and even a book of songs. In *Dimestore* she writes gratefully of her three years in Kentucky: "My involvement with this program made me remem-ber what reading and writing were all about in the first place" (107). Presum-ably, Smith's collaboration with so many talented, yet unpublished, writers strengthened her already substantial commitment to featuring the voices of unrecognized artists in her fiction; the success of her novels and her nearly two-decades-long professorship at North Carolina State University gave her the professional stability to do so.

In 1981 Smith and her first husband, the poet and teacher James Seay, divorced. Her mother, Gig Smith, died after a long illness in 1988, and Ernest Smith followed—"on the last day of his [dimestore's] going-out-of-business sale"—in 1992 (*Dimestore* 20). Gig Smith's illness coincided with the onset of schizophrenia in Smith's younger son, Joshua Seay; "Josh" died from heart issues related to his illness in 2003 at the age of thirty-three. In *Dimestore* Smith movingly explains how writing her fiction, and the novels *Fair and Tender Ladies* and *On Agate Hill*, in particular, kept her afloat through loss. Of *Fair and Tender Ladies,* she has said: "I don't know what I would have done if I hadn't been writing that novel; . . . it was like an open door to another world, another place for me to be for a little while" (177). Smith writes similarly about *On Agate Hill,* written as what she calls "vocational rehabilitation" in the months following her son's death. "Molly's spitfire grit strengthened me," she recalls. "I could laugh" (180). As with events from her girlhood, the stuff of Smith's adult life also is directly present in her fiction. Her son's spirit imbues a character in *On Agate Hill,* and the mental illness focus of *Guests on Earth* grew out of Smith's experience with her parents' and son's hospitalizations and treatments.

While the cultural work Smith has undertaken in her novels and stories has undeniably been serious, it also is ultimately joyful. From her relatively pessimistic early works, Smith developed to write fiction that is lively even when it is bittersweet. Her embrace of the tragedy, beauty, and humor of living finds fullest expression in the stories of Ivy Rowe and Molly Petree. "Oh Mary White," the *Agate Hill* heroine muses on her deathbed, "don't you remember how we danced and danced as the storm came on, what did we know then of lightning?" After a childhood spent among the ghosts of war, the death of her philandering but much-loved husband, and too many lost babies to bear, Molly owns all that has been hers. "I am glad I gave all my heart. . . . I would do it again," she writes (359).

Oral History, Fair and Tender Ladies, and *On Agate Hill* have garnered critical praise and achieved popular success; they also incorporate Smith's most prevalent themes and stylistic motifs. Though the first and the last of these novels are separated in publication by more than twenty years, all are distinguished by their historical scope and expert use of voice. The clear evolution of Smith's voice and focus becomes evident over time. In Smith's works from 1968 to 1980, for instance, she focuses almost exclusively on young female protagonists, aging them slightly from girlhood to young womanhood in her first four novels, respectively. By the 1980s and 1990s, however, Smith consistently was writing family or individual sagas that spanned generations, occasionally following women characters for the entirety of their lives.

The 1968 publication of *The Last Day the Dogbushes Bloomed* took place just after Smith graduated from Hollins College. It is connected with *Something in the Wind* (1971), *Fancy Strut* (1973), and *Black Mountain Breakdown* (1980), works in which Smith plumbs the contradictions of mother-daughter relationships, identity, sexuality, and community for girls and women in the contemporary South. Written mostly from the perspectives of young female characters, these novels are among Smith's most classifiably "Southern," as they deal more with issues of race and less with Appalachian traditions than do her later works. Read chronologically, these novels suggest Smith's growing frustration with roles and choices she perceived as available for young women, particularly in the upper-middle-class South. By 1980, the time of *Black Mountain Breakdown,* Smith had moved her protagonists from disillusionment tempered by vague hope to unhealthy resignation to catatonia. Though the novels lack the formal inventiveness that would come to characterize Smith's mature work, they contain sections of strong narration, in which Smith successfully channels the first-person voices of her narrators.

Oral History marks a turning point in Smith's career. The family saga was her first to include multiple first-person narrators and to incorporate significant amounts of mountain history and folklore. It also was the first of Smith's novels to achieve major critical recognition. As Smith records the tumultuous history of the Cantrell family and their home at Hoot Owl Holler, she addresses the complexity of recording and/or defining history. Smith uses *Oral History*'s formal structure to comment on "the past" as a theme. She has also examined myth and religion, as well as social and racial others. Mothers, in particular, are a central focus of *Oral History,* despite the infrequent use of their own narrative voices.

In the 1988 novel *Fair and Tender Ladies,* Smith chronicles the post-adolescent life of Ivy Rowe, a prolific letter writer from the Virginia mountains. Ivy's impassioned missives and love of language provide windows to her identity, which develops over the course of her relatively long life. Much of Ivy's existence is spent at her childhood home on Sugar Fork; thus, geography and space also are key to understanding Ivy's personal subjectivity. Smith presents ties in *Fair and Tender Ladies* between spirituality and sexuality; Smith expands, here, on the spiritual motifs that she began to plumb in *Black Mountain Breakdown, Oral History,* and *Something in the Wind.*

Publications that have occurred since Smith's shift to writing about families, communities, and women living in the mountains include *The Devil's Dream* (1992), *Saving Grace* (1995), *The Christmas Letters* (1996), and stories from *Me and My Baby View the Eclipse* (1990) and *News of the Spirit* (1997). *The Devil's Dream* is an ambitious chronicle of the history of country music, told through the century-long history of the Bailey family. A family saga with formal similarities to *Oral History,* the novel brings Smith's interest in music to the forefront of her fiction for the first time. In *Saving Grace* Smith treats religion similarly as she narrates the story of a woman searching for religious fulfillment after a traumatic childhood at the hands of her wild evangelist father. Another family is the focus of Smith's more sentimental novella, *The Christmas Letters.* Through three generations of women in the same family, Smith offers a slight but moving commentary on female interdependence and subjectivity. Although the settings and plots of these novels are diverse, the works are linked together by Smith's characteristic channeling of characters' nuanced voices and, usually, weaving together of multiple perspectives to create a fully realized story. In a positive sense of the word Smith's novels published after 1981 are formulaic; in them Smith applies similar literary strategies to vastly different worlds, refining a style that continues to define her career.

Smith's most recent novel, *Guests on Earth* (2013), can be grouped with *Family Linen* (1985) and *The Last Girls* (2002), works in which female mental illness and its treatment are closely examined. The first of these works, *Family Linen*, focuses on a family's response to a murder in their past, though most of the book's action takes place in contemporary Virginia. Smith's themes are similar in *The Last Girls*, which centers on four college suitemates who reunite decades after graduation. Tasked with spreading the ashes of "Baby" Ballou, their enchanting but depressive friend, each woman grapples with both her current challenges and lingering memories. Though separated by decades, these novels resonate with *Guests on Earth*. The generalized anxiety, depression, and repression in *Family Linen* and *The Last Girls* are complemented by the more intense illnesses depicted in *Guests on Earth*, which include schizophrenia and pyromania, among others. Taken together, these novels suggest the challenges mental illness poses to self-knowledge, female subjectivity, and social interaction.

On Agate Hill is a novel in which Smith combines familiar techniques from her writing career with a markedly different historical context. Published in 2006, *On Agate Hill* is the story of Molly Petree, a Civil War–era orphan who begins and ends her life on a crumbling North Carolina plantation. Though the novel includes sections set in Smith's familiar mountains, its physical and ideological context is the postbellum South. *On Agate Hill* also is the most formally ambitious novel Smith has written. Here she fictionalizes letters, diary entries, court records, and song lyrics for use as historical documents, telling Molly's story through a multitude of different sources. In *On Agate Hill* Smith also returns to familiar thematic territory, calling attention to largely untold stories, mother-daughter relationships, and the potential relationship of literacy to identity for women.

CHAPTER 2

I Don't Know What I Can Do Yet
Smith's Early Fiction

Reflecting on her early career in *Dimestore*, Lee Smith is frank about the extent to which she relied on her personal experience for writing material. Of *The Last Day the Dogbushes Bloomed* and *Something in the Wind*, both of which were published by the time she was twenty-seven years old, Smith says: "I had used up my childhood, I had used up my adolescence, and I had nothing more to say. I had used up my whole life!" (166). A job as a reporter helped Smith make the "necessary imaginative leap" to create worlds outside of her own experience, but she continued to work through issues of identity, maternity, sexuality, and community in her next two novels, *Fancy Strut* and *Black Mountain Breakdown* (167). For characters from *The Last Day the Dogbushes Bloomed* to *Black Mountain Breakdown,* these issues are sources of frustration and friction, more obstacle than opportunity. Before Smith could render the relatively fulfilled women of her later novels, she had to grapple with the Susan Tobeys and Crystal Spanglers taking up space in her writerly imagination.

Of Smith's first four novels, three are centered on the lives of young women. *The Last Day the Dogbushes Bloomed, Something in the Wind,* and *Black Mountain Breakdown* convey the stories of progressively older females struggling to define themselves in the face of stifling social norms and personal trauma. While the communities that Susan Tobey, Brooke Kincaid, and Crystal Spangler, respectively, inhabit are a significant presence in each novel, the young women are either first-person narrators of their stories or the tight focus of a third-person narrator. The outlier among Smith's first four novels is *Fancy Strut*, a biting portrait of a small southern town that offers the third-person narratives of many characters. Lucinda MacKethan has connected *Fancy Strut* with the other three novels by calling it a town's coming-of-age story. "Underneath the ridicule of pretense and pride," she argues, "we catch a mood of elegy, striking here for the child the town once was" ("Artists and Beauticians" 6). It also is true that the narratives within *Fancy Strut* are concerned with the subjectivity of individual characters, even as the novel as a whole takes a wider view. The high school outcast Bevo Cartwright, for instance, searches for a way to win the popular girl next door. Unable to conceive of a socially appropriate way to do it, he instead expresses his sexual frustration by setting fire to the high school football stadium. Like Susan Tobey and Brooke Kincaid, Bevo Cartwright has difficulty operating within the social constraints that surround him and struggles to find a satisfying alternative to them.

As Smith's early protagonists form and explore their identities, they frequently act in response to their mothers, who loom large in Smith's first novels. Although later works by Smith contain perspectives of mothers and daughters alike, she writes almost exclusively from the daughters' perspectives in the works from *The Last Day the Dogbushes Bloomed* to *Black Mountain Breakdown*. Susan Tobey and Brooke Kincaid both grapple with the overt sensuality of their mothers, while Crystal Spangler is herself sexualized by her mother Lorene, who enters her in beauty pageants and lives vicariously through the recognition her daughter receives. The mothers here are not identical, but each is a force with which Smith's protagonists must come to terms in order to achieve a sense of selfhood. Over the course of *The Last Day the Dogbushes Bloomed,* for instance, Susan stops being awed by her regal mother and begins to realize the complexity of her mother's brave but also selfish affair; already more likely to identify with neighborhood boys than with her ladylike female relatives, Susan allies herself with her father after her mother deserts the family. The filial relationships in Smith's early novels lay the groundwork for her later fuller explorations of maternity and sexuality.

The young protagonists of Smith's first novels also grapple with their own sexuality, which they often encounter paired with violence. Susan and Crystal both are raped as young girls, while Brooke engages in consensual but frequently destructive sex. In *Fancy Strut* Monica Neighbors begins an affair with a man she despises—she once refers to him as a "lousy little two-bit queer"—out of little more than boredom (62). From Susan to Brooke and Monica, Smith's characters progressively exert more control in their sexual encounters, though that control does not lead them to fulfilling romantic relationships. With Crystal, however, this relatively positive trend reverses; her rape leads to her loss of control in other—all—areas of her life. The only significant sexual relationship that is successful in Smith's early novels is between two relatively minor characters, Ruthie and Ron, in *Fancy Strut*. In their ability to combine

sex with conversation, they are a prototype for the fulfilling romantic relationships that appear more often in later works by Smith.

Community is another factor that often is stifling rather than sustaining or
supportive for Smith's young protagonists. The communities in which Smith
dwells in these novels mostly are composed of middle-class white southerners.
African American characters are present on the periphery of these communities
in some works—in *Something in the Wind,* they pack suitcases, carry luggage,
and play music at frat parties—and central to their lives in others. In *The Last
Day the Dogbushes Bloomed,* Susan is fascinated by Elsie Mae, her family's
maternal housekeeper, and by Frank, the Tobeys' defiant handyman. Though
Frank comes and goes, Elsie Mae is intimately entwined with Susan; she is
almost always at the house, and she is the only person there who honestly considers Susan's many questions. African American characters and white characters in Smith's early novels usually are brought together through financial
exchanges that grant white characters control of the relationships. Elsie Mae
may be an essential source of support for Susan, but her mother, 'the Queen',
holds the power to severe their connection by dismissing Elsie anytime she
pleases. The transactional nature of black and white relationships in Smith's
early books underscores the artifice that limits her fictional communities.

With inadequate parental guidance and deficient community support,
Smith's young characters have little aid when they face trauma; at the end of
each of Smith's first three novels no protagonist seems positioned for a positive outcome. The difference in resolutions for characters in Smith's earlier and
later novels has led many critics to label the early novels as pessimistic relative
to the later ones. "At this point in her writing career," Linda Byrd Cook writes,
"Smith . . . viewed the possibilities for female lives as extremely limited" (9).
Hill, in her book *Lee Smith,* puts it more specifically when she writes, "Smith's
vision darkens until the implicit terminus is reached in *Black Mountain Breakdown* when the protagonist succumbs to catatonia" (30). Smith has affirmed,
to a degree, the suppositions of Cook and Hill in various interviews, but she
also suggests that, as she matured, she felt more confident writing about phases
of life besides young adulthood. "I think that there's something to . . . the
idea that as you get older what comes to interest you is *whole* lives" (Tate 15).
Smith began to practice writing about phases of life besides young womanhood
in *Fancy Strut,* which presents the perspectives of characters besides Monica
Neighbors. Mamaw, for instance, is Bevo Carrtwright's free-spirited and
confident grandmother, a woman who speaks her mind and pursues her interest. A "real card," Mamaw "wore long, full dresses with lots of pockets and
stayed outside all day long" (47). She runs a thriving gardening business in her
daughter's backyard and is quick to laugh at the relatively trivial troubles her

grandchildren encounter. Although she is a minor character, Mamaw illustrates Smith's early ideas about positive possibilities for female characters.

As Smith refined her ideas in her early fiction, she also experimented with formal possibilities. In *The Last Day the Dogbushes Bloomed* and *Something in the Wind,* Smith convincingly writes in the first-person voices of her young narrators. In *Fancy Strut,* however, she attempted a narrative strategy that has come to characterize much of her oeuvre. Smith writes from the viewpoint of many different characters in that novel, presenting a polyvocal take on events in the town. Using a limited third-person voice for most sections, she presents individualized stories without actually writing in specific characters' voices. Smith does this again, to an extent, in *Black Mountain Breakdown.* While Crystal is the tight focus of the novel, Smith's third-person narrator occasionally reveals the perspective of characters such as Crystal's mother, Lorene, and best friend, Agnes. It was not until Smith's next novel, *Oral History,* that she combined first-person narration with the perspectives of multiple characters, channeling many voices to tell her story.

Her formal experimentation is obvious in the tone of Smith's earliest published fiction, too; *Fancy Strut,* particularly, shows how Smith was working to strike a balance between criticism of and empathy for some of her characters. Her critiques in that novel are especially biting, so much so that Hill has called *Fancy Strut* "a cynical and disillusioned book" that offers "a dark view of the human community" (35). Smith herself argues, however, that she sought to gently satirize "human foibles that you also have to love" (Tate 23). Disagreement about the tone of Smith's novel suggests the work she was doing to develop her own writerly voice.

Identity

Though characters in much of Smith's fiction are uncelebrated artists, her earliest protagonists are not primarily concerned with expressing themselves through art. Susan Tobey and Crystal Spangler, for instance, both dabble in poetry but neither seriously pursues writing; they have vaguely artistic temperaments with little direction. The protagonists of Smith's first four novels are young girls and women in search of ways to define themselves and express themselves authentically in relationships. As they pursue self-knowledge and understanding, Smith's protagonists often find it difficult to reconcile their imaginative inner lives with the realities of the worlds around them. Carmen Rueda Ramos describes this difficulty by using a mirror, an image prominently featured in *Black Mountain Breakdown.* Susan, Brooke Kinkaid, and Crystal, she argues "try to discover whether they should define themselves through the cultural values of the looking glass or instead break the mirror of repetition to search for their true [identities] and [new] language with which to express [them]" (43). Though Ramos does not extend her metaphor to *Fancy Strut*, it applies to parts of that novel, too; characters such as Monica Neighbors maintain public appearances that do not reflect their honest thoughts and feelings. The conflict between interiority and exteriority that these early protagonists encounter frequently stops them from acting on their impulses; passivity becomes their default response to challenges.

Smith's protagonists often use comparison to their families or peers as a way to measure their identities. Susan, for instance, compares her appearance to her sister's as she considers what her role she might have in her "royal" family. Her feet, she thinks, "looked like boy feet when they were next to the Princess' princess feet in those shaky shoes . . . . Mine were brown and flat and looked like Robert's" (39). Susan identifies herself with a neighborhood boy rather than the regal women of her family and ultimately sees herself as a subject rather than a member of the Queen's court. Susan's lack of identification with her family leads her to seek closer companionship with her neighborhood friends, animals she watches at a pond, and Elsie Mae, the family's housekeeper. As she considers her identity in relation to that of each new companion, Susan reaches a striking conclusion about her integrated place in the world. "I prayed to the grass and to the flowers and to the rocks and to everything," she marvels, laughing; "it was all the same. . . . It was all the same" (179). Though Susan has not fully formed her identity at the end of summer, she has come to recognize the interconnectedness of the world she inhabits. Her new awareness of life and mortality—"everything was dying and . . . then I knew that I was too," she thinks—gives her a new lens through which she can continue to gain self-knowledge (180).

When Smith's early protagonists compare themselves to others, they frequently end up feeling as if their identities are fragmented. Smith repeats motifs of fragmentation in each of her first four novels, underscoring its centrality to her ideas about the search for self-knowledge. While Susan "fixed [her] mind up so it was cut into boxes" to avoid thinking upsetting thoughts, Brooke is compelled by her comparisons to try and split herself in two (173). "One half belonged to Brooke Kincaid, the daughter of Mr. and Mrs. T. Royce Kincaid of River Bend, a recent graduate of St. Dominique's School," she explains. "The other half belonged to me. I was real, and the other half was only apparent" (31). Monica, who is older than either Susan or Brooke, thinks with less abstraction about her split self. When her husband hands her a drink, she recalls, "she had smiled and thanked him and suddenly, unaccountably, she had felt like an imposter" (32). Brooke's insecurities are more concrete. In *Black Mountain Breakdown* Crystal's very name evokes her multifaceted identity, which constantly changes depending on her company. As Cook puts it, "she must stand beside or opposite something to gain any substance at all" (47). Crystal, the last of Smith's early protagonists, is also the least integrated.

In these early novels language is the primary signifier of Smith's characters' (in)abilities to express their authentic selves. Characters who cannot verbalize their thoughts generally feel disconnected from their families and communities and question the validity of their developing identities. Brooke, for instance, looks to textual sources as varied as *Ripley's Believe It or Not,* crossword puzzles, Victorian literature, and the Bible in an effort to find a discourse to adopt. Unsatisfied with all of them, she tells her boyfriend, "I'd like to make up a whole new language" (181). Instead, Brooke continually varies her handwriting—"I was always interested to see how I would write," she says—trying on new identities every time she lifts a pen (201). Her seeming lack of control over which handwriting will appear on the page suggests the degree to which Brooke ultimately feels clueless about which font truly is hers. Smith revisits the metaphor of handwriting for identity in *Black Mountain Breakdown,* in which Crystal, whose identity is even less stable than Brooke's, "can't fix upon a handwriting. She writes a different way each day" (48). Smith underscores the connection between literacy and identity through Brooke and Crystal, beginning an exploration that spans her career to date.

The critic Margaret Homans speaks to the universality of Brooke's struggles with language in her essay "'Her Very Own Howl': The Ambiguities of Representation in Recent Women's Fiction." For women, Homans argues, "there is a specifically gender-based alienation from language that is characterized by the special ambiguity of women's simultaneous participation in and exclusion from a hegemonic group" (205). While Brooke is a white woman in the twentieth-century South, and thus afforded greater hegemony than, for instance, her African American peers, she remains subject to patriarchal institutions—family, church, fraternity and sorority codes, to name a few—that influence her identity. In her attempts to negotiate this ambiguity Brooke illustrates both "[women's] ambivalence concerning appropriation of the dominant discourse" and "their ambivalence about what alternatives to this discourse might exist" (Homans 191). As she writes about the likes of Brooke and Crystal, especially, Smith's perspective on the possibilities that both dominant and alternative discourses represent for young women is grim. However, Smith's own success in using language expressively as a woman—though less assured in her early works of fiction—provides a hopeful counterexample to the situations about which she writes. Smith is a writer who, as Homans puts it, "formally duplicate[s] the female experience that [she] thematize[s], the experience of both participating in and standing outside the dominant culture" (205).

Erica Abrams Locklear has written more specifically about literacy's relationship to identity for young women in Appalachia. For Appalachian women in particular, she argues, "gaining new literacies never happens easily," because it "often results in the constant negotiation of self-identity." Locklear sites the "fear of 'getting above their raisings,' a phrase characterized by alienation from family and home culture as a result of literacy attainment," as a primary challenge for Appalachian women acquiring literacy (2). Though Smith's engagement with this problem is more noticeable in her later, Appalachian-set fiction, she sets the stage for that engagement in her early novels. Crystal, especially, is rebuked when she tries to gain self-knowledge by reading the diary of her ancestor, Emma Turlington Field. Crystal's husband, Roger Lee Combs, "takes the journal from her lap and closes it and puts it in the fire" (233). Crystal was not gaining much self-knowledge from the diary, but its removal is the catalyst that causes her to give up on knowing herself, entirely. John D. Kalb has gone so far as to call Roger Lee's action a "second rape" of Crystal, a violation by which he convinces her that she has nothing empowering on which to draw (28). Shortly after Roger Lee burns the journal, "Crystal paralyzes herself. She just stops moving. She stops talking, stops doing everything" (237). Without a defined identity to guide her choices, Crystal becomes completely passive.

The passivity to which Crystal so dramatically succumbs is, to varying degrees, the end result of unsuccessful attempts at self-knowledge depicted in Smith's first novels. The older Smith's early protagonists are, the more passive they are at the end of their narratives. While Susan ends her summer resigned to the presence of evil in the world, Brooke comes "full circle" and can see vague "new directions" for her life by the close of *Something in the Wind* (243). Monica, however, returns to her unfulfilling marriage after her affair in *Fancy Strut,* determined to have a baby because of her need for "something totally new" (299). Susan and Brooke are optimistic despite being unresolved, but Monica's seeming decisiveness is so shallow as to be comical. Crystal's passivity is the most severe by design; when she began *Black Mountain Breakdown* Smith "decided to write a book about this tendency that women, particularly Southern women in my generation, have to be passive" (Tate 32). By making Crystal Spangler her representative of passivity, Smith roots that trait in race and class as well as in geography. Crystal specifically is symbolic of white middle-class femininity," which Beverley Skeggs has called "the ideal but also . . . the most passive and dependent" of twentieth-century femininities (129). Though Crystal is not Lee Smith's last passive character, she is her most extreme.

Maternity and Sexuality

The mothers and daughters in Smith's first four novels do not spend much time discussing sexuality with one another. When they do broach the topic, they usually obscure it in euphemisms and platitudes about acceptable standards of behavior. For the daughters, whose perspectives are central in these early works, these silences lead to discomfort with the idea of their mothers as sexual women and confusion about their own sexuality. The divided identities that Smith's early protagonists sometimes cultivate are reflected in their experiences with sex. While protagonists such as Brooke and Monica seek out sex, they also each seek to separate their minds from their bodies during intercourse, holding back from their partners even as they are physically intimate. Susan and Crystal attempt to maintain a similar split between their minds and bodies in sexual situations more traumatic; both experience rape at a young age. We cannot know the long-term effects of Susan's violation by Eugene, but Crystal's rape by her handicapped uncle, Devere, reverberates for decades of her life. Whether consensual or not, intercourse entails varying degrees of pain for the protagonists of Smith's early fiction.

When the mothers in these novels advise their daughters, it most frequently is on standards of ladylike behavior and appearance; they are ineffectual mentors when their daughters raise substantial questions. The Queen, for instance, deflects Susan's earnest inquiries about relationships by brushing them off and changing the subject to her daughter's often-unkempt appearance. When Susan overhears her mother admitting that she married Susan's father because she became pregnant, she tries to understand how that could happen. "Instead of addressing Susan's questions, The Queen scolds her for allowing her rain-soaked clothes to drip on the floor. "Oh, *look* what you've done to the rug," the Queen responds. "Susan, go upstairs this minute and put on some dry clothes" (109). The Queen also can be cruel instead of simply dismissive. When Susan worries about menstruation, she laughs at her and repeats Susan's concerns to a friend. As Cook writes, "Susan's first sexual knowledge, delivered to her by her mother, is coupled with misunderstanding and embarrassment" (21). Carolyn Kincaid, too, has little in the way of helpful advice for her confused daughter. "'You ought to go out every weekend but you shouldn't go out two nights in a row with the same boy,'" she tells Brooke. "'One thing you have got to remember . . . is that boys don't like pale little egghead girls'" (33). Rather than giving her daughter useful information about sex and relationships, Carolyn instructs Brooke only on how to attract male attention. Though both the

Queen and Carolyn are sources of comedy in their narratives, they are of little use when their daughters are in trouble.

A product of western Virginia, Crystal Spangler's mother, Lorene, is less concerned with ladylike behavior than the Queen or Carolyn. She also is less aloof than those mothers and is a hands-on presence in Crystal's life. Still, her involvement consists of mostly kind but superficial care; Lorene fixates on Crystal's physical appearance and works to maintain her daughter's beauty. Her ineffectuality is illustrated when Crystal mourns a breakup. Lorene wants to find out what happened and advise her daughter. Instead, though, she "applies spray starch to the ruffle [on Crystal's dress] and it comes out perfect, and Lorene wishes that Crystal herself was this easy to straighten out" (113). A pragmatist, Lorene does not feel capable of engaging her dreamy, moody daughter; as Minrose Gwin puts it, she "takes what comes and doesn't ask hard questions" ("Nonfelicitous Space" 93). That Crystal's moodiness is a trait she shares with her father, Lorene's estranged husband Grant, only hampers Lorene's attempts to connect with her daughter. Her decades of frustration with Grant and, to a lesser extent, with Crystal's older brothers, have stripped Lorene of confidence in her ability to understand her family members. Lorene's shallow involvement extends to Crystal's sex life. Though she monitors her comings and goings with boys—"'I expect you home by twelve,'" she warns Crystal before she leaves on a date—Lorene does not speak frankly about love and relationships (95). Crystal has her mother's attention but not her guidance.

Because their mothers are so consumed with staid appearances, Smith's protagonists sometimes are confused when their mothers are sexualized. They are not alone. As Marianne Hirsch has argued, although "nothing entangles women more firmly in their bodies than pregnancy, birth, lactation, miscarriage, or the inability to conceive, ...the connection of maternity and sexuality remains a pervasive taboo in feminist analysis" (166). Susan offers the strongest embodiment of this taboo in Smith's work; when she discovers her father's sensual paintings of her mother, she is fascinated but also uncomfortable. The paintings make her feel like "sin in the Bible," and she especially is bothered by a portrait of the Queen with her mouth open and eyes rolled back (70). "I knew it was awful but it was beautiful too," she thinks. "That messed me up" (119). Susan's complicated feelings about the paintings are foregrounded when, a few days earlier, she looks at book of nude portraits with her friends; "I wished I had that green book for my very own and then I was glad I didn't," she thinks (97). Susan knows that the paintings of her mother are connected with the nude portraits, an association that makes her uneasy, but which she lacks information and vocabulary to understand.

Susan's confusion about her mother as a sexual figure is damaging, but it does help her imagine expanded possibilities for middle-class white women. As Smith said in an interview with Ramos, "Susan makes up the whole myth that her mother has been a Queen in order to put her mother up on . . . the mythic scale, where it is OK to be on a quest, which it is not in their own lives" (70). The Queen refuses to play by the rules of marriage, church, and other institutions, and Susan claims to feel lucky just to know such an unconventional woman. Through her resistance to convention, the Queen combats "the idea that motherhood and creative expression cannot coexist within the individual woman," which Paula Gallant Eckard calls a pervasive obstacle for female expression (*Maternal Body* 24). That the Queen's bravery leads to Susan's heartbreak creates a tension in *The Last Day the Dogbushes Bloomed*. Female agency and maternity are in conflict, here. The Queen's dilemma is central even as her voice is absent; she and her daughter each suffer as the Queen leaves a maternal role to which she feels ill suited.

If Smith's early protagonists feel conflicted about their mothers' sexualization, they are even more confused, and sometimes traumatized, by their own sexual experiences. Because of this confusion Brooke and Monica try to separate physical intimacy from emotional or mental involvement. Brooke, for instance, thinks about her body in the third person when she kisses her deceased friend's brother, John Howard. "Do what you will with Brooke's body," she thinks, "but please stay out of her mind" (40). Monica, too, takes her self out of the action when she kisses Buck Fire, the actor with whom she pursues an affair. "Who," she wonders as they fool around in an airplane, "was this strange sky girl, practically wetting her pants?" (143). In large part Brooke and Monica try to remove some essential part of themselves from their sexual experiences to absolve themselves of guilt. In Monica's case her guilt is attributable to her deceased mother. "Monica had learned . . . during her careful bringing-up" that "there are certain occupational types with whom nice girls don't associate" (62). Brooke's guilt is less obvious but tied up with her feelings about Charles, John Howard's deceased brother and Brooke's best friend. "I had never kissed anybody before in my life," she thinks as she makes out with John Howard, "not even Charles" (39).

Brooke and Monica also act in response to social standards that they are resigned to uphold when they try to separate their thoughts from their sexual actions. The critic Kathryn Lee Seidel has written about the sort of world each inhabits. "A society that prefers its lovely young women to be charming and flirtatious coquettes who never yield their purity," she observes, "can create a situation of impossible tension for the belle: she is asked to exhibit herself as sexually desirable to the appropriate males, yet she must not herself respond sexually" (xvi). Smith illustrates this reality in her fiction when Monica repeat-edly mentions her shame at having been promiscuous during a trip to Europe and when Brooke dares to initiate sex with her fraternity boyfriend, Houston. Though he has no problem approaching Brooke for sex, he balks when she tries to pull him down in the snow, saying "come on, come on, come on." "'What is the matter with you?'" he asks. "'What the hell is wrong?'" (99). Instead of appreciating Brooke's desire for him, Houston pulls her back to the cabin, call-ing off their relationship soon after the incident.

Brooke has a healthier sexual relationship with her next boyfriend, Bentley, but is surprised to find that his ideas about women are not so different from Houston's. While Bentley does not mind Brooke's sexual assertiveness, he applies a different word—*whore*—to promiscuous women than he does to men who frequently have sex. "'Girls are different,'" he says; "'Guys can do what they want to'" (196). Their relationship begins to crumble the same night that Brooke questions his double standard; their apartment begins to shake, and Brooke thinks she sees an ominous "gray shape" standing in their doorway (197). These unexplained, metaphysical disturbances are a manifestation of the problems threatening Brooke and Bentley's relationship. Similar juxtapositions of sex with physical violence or danger recur in Smith's early fiction. Earlier in *Something in the Wind*, for instance, Brooke aims a shotgun at Bentley when he tells her he loves her; in *Fancy Strut* Monica wishes her husband would "rip off her Tanner dress so violently that the buttons would sound like bullets as they hit the wall, and throw her down upon the floor" (185). Brooke and Monica, respectively, create and desire violence in their sexual relationships.

For Susan and Crystal sexual violence is a traumatic reality rather than something they seek. Their long-term responses to their rapes, though, resemble Brooke's and Monica's responses to intercourse; each young girl tries to trick her mind into forgetting about her besieged body. Susan feels excruciatingly present in her body during her rape by Eugene—"the Iron Lung was hurting me between my legs," she says, "and the dirt was coming from all around to cover me . . . because I was dying"—but later tries to file the hurt away in an inacces-sible compartment of her brain (163). Crystal, too, feels intense pain when her uncle, Devere, rapes her. However, Smith represses the rape for readers as she does for Crystal; the novel reveals only the barest of details about the rape when it actually occurs in the narrative. "Devere comes and pushes her down on the cold dirt floor," the novel reads, "and the wrench drops at last from his hand. Later Crystal can never remember this or anything about it" (68). Aside from a few scattered mentions of Crystal having menstrual-like cramps and feeling ill, these lines are the most direct reference to her rape until much later in the novel, sixteen years later in Crystal's life. It is only when Crystal's memories of the event come rushing back that readers have a fuller, horrifying window into what has happened. The hurt, Crystal thinks, "seems to be traveling up her whole body into her shoulders and then pinpointing itself somewhere up at the very top of her head" (229).

The narrator's and Crystal's initial silences about Crystal's rape initially make it hard to discern the effects of sexual violence on her life. As Gwin has argued, "the reader must create a story out of Crystal's silence" ("Nonfelicitous Space" 91). Crystal's family is silent, too, in response to her rape, because no one ever realizes that it has happened. In Susan's case, however, adults do not adequately address her rape despite her insistence, in the only vocabulary she has to describe it, that it occurred. "'Aren't you going to do anything to me?'" she asks the parents of her friends. "'I hurt down there. What about that?'" Susan is persistent, continuing to seek recognition when her friend's mother answers with a pat and throwaway assertion that all will be well. "'It's not all right,'" she says. "'What're you going to do?'" In response to her persistence Susan's community firmly demands her silence. "'Hush, Susan,' they said. 'It's all right'" (170). Even rape does not change Susan's community's habit of brushing off her attempts to gain knowledge. The silencing of Crystal and Susan underscores the extent to which language and speech impact their developing subjectivities. If the idea of discourse as a signifier of identity seems abstract, here Susan and Crystal's inabilities to communicate with adults in their communities are tragically concrete.

The one adult who does communicate extensively with Crystal about matters besides her appearance is Grant Spangler, her alcoholic, couch-ridden father. Grant is able to tap into Crystal's love of stories and language in a way that no one else she knows can; she spends hours by his side as he reads poetry and recites fables for her in the darkened parlor he occupies. As Caren J. Town notes, Crystal's father provides her with a "link to literature [and] the past" (31). However, Grant's physical similarity to Devere, as well as the pleasure he takes in Crystal's frightened responses to his stories, lends a disturbing subtext to their father-daughter interactions. Gwin outlines the "obvious erotic implications" to a scene in which Grant reads Crystal "The Spider and the Fly"—"the seductive story, the father's seductive reading, the daughter's fear and pleasure" (91). When Grant dies Crystal is the one who finds him; he expires the day after her rape by Devere. The timing of these two tragedies inextricably ties Crystal's positive memories of her father to her violation by her uncle, though Crystal does not consciously recognize the link. Her memory goes silent along with Grant's storytelling voice.

While each of the main characters in Smith's early novels has a damaging and violent exposure to intercourse, peripheral characters fare better, offering alternatives to the bleak experiences of Smith's protagonists. *Fancy Strut* offers the greatest concentration of these, as it is told from the third-person limited perspectives of many residents of Speed. Sandy and Sharon Dubois, for instance, a mother and daughter in that novel, are both comfortable sexually asserting themselves. Sharon masturbates in her mirror, directly contradicting the self-effacing power of mirrors in the lives of Smith's early protagonists. Sandy, Sharon's mother, is even more transgressive. "Sandy's wild laughter," Cook argues, "sets her apart from other women as she disrupts the status quo in her extramarital affair" (40). The confident, self-assured quartet of Sandy, Sharon, Ruthie, and Mamaw, all of whom live on the same block, offers a striking contrast to Monica and her lack of self-knowledge and sexual fulfillment. In Smith's later fiction women who own their sexual desires will be the protagonists of their own stories. Throughout her first four novels, though, they are relegated to experimental subplots.

Communities

As the protagonists of Smith's first four novels try to establish their identities, they necessarily respond to the communities that surround them. They most commonly react against the norms of these communities, positioning themselves as outsiders in a world of artifice. Composed mostly of middle-class white southerners, towns such as Speed, Alabama, the setting of *Fancy Strut,* are also home to small numbers of African American characters, many of whom work in the homes of white families. Smith's fictionalization of the relationships between her white female protagonists and the African American workers whom they encounter is unique in her career. While no African American character narrates a section of these early novels, several have significant dialogue; in *The Last Day the Dogbushes Bloomed,* for instance, Elsie Mae speaks nearly as much as the Queen. Still, this dialogue always is filtered through white narrators, who occasionally position themselves against their families or communities on issues of race. Brooke and her brother, Carter, reject their mother's casual racism, while Lloyd Warner of *Fancy Strut* enjoys legally representing African American students in his town against his rival, the town mayor. *Black Mountain Breakdown,* however, features no intimate interaction between African American and white characters. The novel is typical of Smith's Appalachian-set fiction in its lack of black characters.

When the mothers in Smith's early fiction compel their daughters to behave in ladylike ways, it often is because they fear community censure. Though Crystal's mother is less concerned with decorum than the Queen or Carolyn, she still worries about what her peers think of Crystal's behavior. When Crystal breaks up with her high school boyfriend Roger Lee, for instance, Lorene angrily lectures her: "I don't understand how you can just up and do something like that!" What Lorene thinks, but doesn't say to Crystal, is that her daughter's actions will have a ripple effect within their small community. "Lorene also can't figure out," the narrator reveals, "how she can ever face Roger's mother again if she happens to run into her in the Piggly Wiggly or on the street" (86). Brooke notices her older sister Liz entertaining similar concerns at her friend Charles's funeral. When Brooke asks questions during a hymn, Liz angrily tells her to "shut up and sing." "If I had been one of her kids," Brooke thinks, "she would have smacked my hand" (16). Liz's anger is roused because Brooke is not blending in with the community of churchgoers. The incredulity and anger that communities express when a young woman does not fulfill her prescribed role are frequently reenacted in Smith's early novels.

When Susan and her ilk reject standards of the ladylike roles their communities expect them to fill, it is often because they find those roles inauthentic. Brooke, especially, positions her "real" self in opposition to the falseness she perceives in her communities. At Charles's wake she is aghast at the normal conversations people carry on near his coffin. "The other people in the kitchen talked softly about everything under the sun: the governor, crops, their children, the new Episcopal priest, a divorce," she observes. "How can they do this with Charles in the next room?" (11). Lloyd Warner, a lawyer in *Fancy Strut,* provides a male perspective on the artifice of ladylike roles when he thinks about his mother. "She had played the grande dame all her life," he muses. "Nothing so preposterous as her husband's suicide was going to strip her of her role" (233). The friction generated by characters in search of authentic selves brushing up against communities that demand conformity sometimes leads to violent confrontation. Lloyd illustrates this best when he shoots himself during a mock–Civil War battle staged at Speed's sesquicentennial. He defies the pageant's artifice by creating a real wound, with real blood, and the pageant soon descends into chaos.

As Lloyd's Civil War scene suggests, Smith's protagonists often see propriety as a particularly Southern demand. When Brooke awkwardly rejects an advance by John Howard, for instance, she thinks: "Sometimes I thought that Brooke wasn't really Southern after all. I knew what she would have done if she was Southern. She would have slapped John Howard's hand . . . and laughed a lot, and then she would have gone to rush" (41). For Brooke, being Southern means maintaining charming femininity at all times; it means following in the footsteps of her "gay young thing" mother, Carolyn, and imitating her sorority-girl college roommate, Diana (31). Lloyd feels unwillingly connected to the Southern past, too. After years in New York, Lloyd cannot quite understand his decision to return to Speed, his hometown. "Only a fool would come back to Speed," he thinks. "He felt at home here, that was all. Faulkner shit" (121). Engaged in a strange dance of attraction and repulsion with his community, Lloyd wears seersucker and plays the eccentric alcoholic even as he hates himself for doing it. His visits to his mother epitomize his conflict. Something unidentifiable, he thinks, "kept him walking over [to her house] every day of his life and hating every minute of it" (234). Like Brooke, who tries to fit into her middle-class white community even as she resents it, Lloyd is compulsively a part of his town.

Susan admires the resistance to her community's norms that is offered up by Frank, her family's African American handyman. When Frank manages to get hired without saying anything more than his first name to the Queen, Susan's mother is angry. "Frank had fixed her good," Susan thinks, and she files the incident away in her mind (31). Later, she watches, fascinated, as Frank shocks her parents by mowing the same patch of lawn over and over again, drunk and singing hymns. "All those years I had thought Frank was the gardener in the palace of the Queen," she thinks, "but he was not that at all. He was something else" (53). Susan begins to understand Frank's existence outside the laws of decorum when he commits fraud to receive aid from the government, a "bigger thing than anything [Susan] knew of except God. But Frank cheated it; . . . I thought he was really brave" (136). Frank's small acts of defiance and independence are inspiring to Susan, who is just beginning to think of ways she can assert her own identity. When Frank suddenly dies, she feels disillusioned and begins to recognize her own mortality. Still, Susan finds even his death to be bold. "He didn't have the right to die but he had done it; . . . that hard green light of dying blew up in me like a flashbulb" (177). Though she never speaks to him, Susan is attracted by Frank's otherness and defiance.

Frank's willfulness threatens the Queen so much because her lifestyle is supported by his compliant labor. The white female identities that are so central in Smith's early novels are partially defined, too, by their dependence on the work of African American women. To be the Queen, for instance, Susan's mother needs servants to perform the household labors that she does not. As Nina Baym writes, "The Southern belle is a princess, idle and free; the Southern matron a queen, always busy, to be sure, but busy with gracious ceremony and elegant appearances" (193). Monica, likewise, is free to attend bridge-club parties and chair the "Sesquicentennial Headquarters Committee" because Suetta, her family's African American housekeeper, is vacuuming the rugs—whether Monica likes it or not. "It was unthinkable to [Monica's husband] Manly that his wife should not have a maid," the narrator explains. "It was a matter of life style" (28). When Monica decides to change her life at the end of *Fancy Strut,* it is significant that dismissing Suetta is the biggest change she makes. Desperate for something, anything, to do, Monica must first be in control of her own home, which entails ending the expectation that someone else will clean it for her.

Smith underscores the discomfort of both the Queen and Monica with their domestic help by describing their reliance on money as a means of control. When Frank drunkenly mows the lawn, for instance, Susan's father unsuccessfully tries to talk him into leaving the Tobeys' property. It is only when Mr. Tobey gives Frank a dollar that he goes, though he sings as loudly as possible as he departs. In a way Frank has manipulated Mr. Tobey just as he does the government; by making his employers uncomfortable—easily done, he knows—Frank gets paid without having to do his work. Monica, likewise, offers Suetta severance pay when the maid shows reluctance to leave the job she has held for decades. "'I'll pay you for two weeks, of course,'" she says, "'until you find another job.'" Monica believes that she can dismiss Suetta by stopping her pay after two weeks, but Suetta feels a more personal connection to her work. "'I'll be talking to Mr. Manly,'" she says before she leaves, thus challenging Monica's ability to fire her (298). Smith never places the reader in Suetta's thoughts, but it seems she views her place in the Neighbors' home as dependent on factors besides financial transactions.

In *The Last Day the Dogbushes Bloomed* the household labors that the Queen passes on to Elsie Mae include caring for Susan, which likewise complicates the housekeeper's relationship to the family. Elsie Mae gives Susan physical sustenance by preparing her meals and washing her clothes, but she also is the only person in Susan's household who tries to answer her earnest questions and tell her truthful stories. The critic Bettina Entzminger points to Elsie Mae's stories as especially crucial for Susan's development. "The black character remains a shadow figure in the works of recent [Southern] women writers," she notes, "but . . . the figure mothers the young writers' repressed creativity struggling to emerge" (160). Susan recognizes and appreciates Elsie Mae's wit. "I was the only one in the castle who knew how smart Elsie Mae was," Susan thinks, recalling an incident in which the Queen made fun of Elsie Mae in front of party guests (111). Susan's recollection binds her to her caretaker; she, too, has been made the object of the Queen's jokes and is smarter than she is given credit for. The young girl's attachment to Elsie Mae is noticeable enough that Susan's older sister Betty attempts to disrupt it. Inventing an excuse to get Susan out of the kitchen, Betty says that "it's not a good idea to spend so much time with the help" (117).

What is less clear in *The Last Day the Dogbushes Bloomed* is the extent of Elsie Mae's attachment to Susan. Entzminger has singled her out as "the traditional southern mammy," and "the opposite of the jezebel [Queen]," which

seems fair given the kisses, laughs, and comfort that fill her interactions with
Susan (159). However, Jocelyn Hazelwood Donlon cautions readers against
assuming too much about a relationship that remains dependent on the financial transactions of others. "In White Southern fiction," she notes, "the Black
teller is frequently sentimentalized as an 'intimate' part of the family—an
image rooted in White plantation fiction where the 'Good Slave' cheerfully
entertains White children by the hour" (20). By fictionalizing relationships
between African American domestic workers and the white families they serve,
Smith participates in a long-standing Southern literary tradition. Harriet
Beecher Stowe's *Uncle Tom's Cabin* (1852), William Faulkner's *The Sound and
the Fury* (1928), Eudora Welty's *Delta Wedding* (1946), Toni Morrison's *The
Bluest Eye* (1970), and Ellen Douglas's *Can't Quit You, Baby* (1988), to name
only a few of many novels, examine relationships like Susan's and Elsie Mae's.

Smith moves her depictions of race relations from the domestic sphere into
the legal one with *Fancy Strut,* which features a racial discrimination lawsuit
as well as a small-scale race riot. In that novel, though, her gentle examination
is replaced by focused satire that does not spare African American or white
characters. While Monica and Suetta stare one another down in the Neighbors'
home, Lloyd Warner helps local African American college students mount a
lawsuit against an apartment complex that refuses to rent to one of them. The
suit is just and exposes some of the behavior on which Speed's white establishment is built, but Smith refuses to make martyrs of the young men bringing the
suit. According to the relatively reliable narration of Lloyd Warner, Chall, the
plaintiff, is entitled and not especially bright; Theolester, who puts his friend
up to the lawsuit, is opportunistic and trying too hard to embody an activist
role. Smith ties together past and present by including a mock–Civil War battle
in Speed's pageant. When Lloyd actually is shot during the display, Theolester
incites a riot downtown; he assumes Lloyd has been targeted because of the
legal action he is undertaking on behalf of the black students. That Lloyd is
responsible for his own wound makes the riot uncomfortably comic—Theolester has cause to revolt against injustice in Speed, but the impetus for his boldest
action is faulty.

After her direct engagement with challenges to Jim Crow policies in
Fancy Strut, Smith began her foray into Appalachian-set fiction and started
to feature fewer African American characters. In *Black Mountain Breakdown*
Crystal's small mountain community is so racially homogenous that the narrator never mentions African Americans until Crystal leaves home. Visiting
Richmond for a beauty pageant, Crystal thinks how "Negroes fascinate her;
there are no Negroes in Black Rock and there's no reason for them to move
there either, Lorene has always said. Nothing to do except work in the mines"

(136). Though Crystal and her mother do not live in close proximity to African Americans, they nonetheless have absorbed cultural ideas about how they should behave around persons of color. "Before they leave the [hotel] room," the narrator relates, "Lorene puts her money into her bra so that it won't be stolen by Negroes" (137). Asides such as this comprise most mentions of African Americans in Smith's fiction from *Black Mountain Breakdown* until *On Agate Hill* (2006), published more than twenty years later. As Donlon has argued, Smith "lead[s] her readers into a distinctive racial and cultural community"; like the Grundy of her youth, Smith's Appalachia is largely inhabited by white characters (29).

Smith's turn to Appalachian communities in *Black Mountain Breakdown* marked a major shift in her career. For her protagonists this turn includes an opportunity to access more supportive communities. In Smith's later novels female characters often find positive identification with their communities rather than pressure to conform. As Katherine Kearns puts it, "Smith's hard-won knowledge" from her early fiction "is channeled into figures of matriarchal power" (176). Grace Shepherd of *Saving Grace* (1995), for instance, feels grounded in her mother's loving and generous variety of Christianity and finds comfort in practicing her mother's traditions. Linda Wagner-Martin argues that nourishing communities of women have been a "constant in a hundred years of the Southern novel by women," noting how female characters "have been—and still are—drawing much of their sustenance and their wisdom from a female line of ancestry, and thereby creating a true community of women" (32). Smith, though, had to move her fiction to Appalachia in order to envision that sort of community. Though Smith's early protagonists desire but do not find communities of supportive women, they pave the way for the women who follow them in Smith's oeuvre.

CHAPTER 3

A Chain of Her Own Choosing or Dreaming
Oral History

While Lee Smith attempted to publish *Black Mountain Breakdown* (1980)—it took, by her reckoning, about eight years—she was raising two sons and writing mostly short stories. She published fourteen of them in her 1981 collection *Cakewalk,* which features contemporary characters living in the rural South. With stories set in places such as Gulfport, Mississippi, and on the beaches of the Carolinas, *Cakewalk* has little that is uniquely Appalachian within its pages, putting it in stark contrast to the novels that Smith would publish later in the decade. *Oral History* (1983), *Family Linen* (1985), and *Fair and Tender Ladies* (1988) are all firmly grounded in the history and the manners of Smith's mountain homeland, a territory she was just beginning to feel she could re-create in her fiction.

The first of those novels, *Oral History,* began as a similarly titled short story. Set in the mountains of western Virginia, the story centers on a young woman who ventures into a holler to record the stories of her estranged relatives. After publishing "Oral History" in the *Carolina Quarterly,* Smith "decided to write the novel filling in what would be on the [recording]," adding the textured voices of dead and living characters from Hoot Owl Holler (Tate 10). The resulting novel, her first major commercial and critical success, established Smith's literary association with the Appalachian present and the folklore of the region's past. While *Oral History* revisits themes familiar from Smith's first four novels—sexuality, motherhood, and young women's searches for identity, to name a few—the novel's dramatically different spatial setting freed Smith to approach those themes from a new angle. Women still struggle to establish identities and resist patriarchal community structures in *Oral*

History, but for the first time in Smith's fiction, some female protagonists find ways to live authentic, powerful, and sexually fulfilled lives.

Oral History opens with the story of Jennifer, a suburban college student completing an oral history project for a course. Visiting her late mother's family for the first time she can remember, Jennifer writes her "Impressions" of them for her project. She also places a tape recorder in the family's ancestral home, which is supposedly haunted by spirits from the Cantrells' tumultuous past. Though Jennifer's writing is affected and not terribly insightful, the voices her tape recorder collects are engaging and illuminating. Beginning with the voice of the community healer, Granny Younger, these voices fill most of Smith's novel, relating three generations of Jennifer's family history.

The center of Granny Younger's tale is Almarine, a handsome man whose romances end disastrously. After taking up with Red Emmy, an older woman reputed to be a witch, Almarine casts her out of his home when she becomes pregnant. His dismissal of Emmy sets in motion a supposed curse that plagues the Cantrell family for generations: Almarine's young wife, Pricey Jane, and young son both die from drinking bad milk; his daughter Dory commits suicide after a heartbreaking life; and his granddaughter Pearl dies in childbirth after an affair with one of her high school students. These events are related by speakers from both inside and outside the family, by characters who reside in the hollers and by "foreigners" with little knowledge of mountain life. In all, thirteen voices combine to reveal the Cantrells' story.

The novel's polyvocal structure creates an aura of myth about the characters' stories, which is reinforced by the subject matter they address. Because so many speakers provide their impression of the Cantrells' history, the novel itself never offers an authoritative version of the past. Instead, readers must sift through and evaluate the evidence characters offer in pursuit of the "true" story, which remains elusive. Rosalind B. Reilly has written about the recurring motif of the circle in *Oral History,* arguing that the novel is founded on a "circular structure . . . mirrored in microcosm throughout the book" (82). Just as the novel begins and ends with the present-day story of Jennifer and her relatives, the voices within the novel tell stories that circle back on one another, creating patterns of both hope and destruction.

For a novel so infused with superstition and mystery, *Oral History* also is markedly grounded, as it grapples with motherhood and the roles of other female caretakers. Granny Younger, for instance, describes Red Emmy as a witch who possesses Almarine, but another story emerges between the lines of what Granny actually says. Emmy works hard on the farm during Almarine's illness, yet the reward for her work is banishment by Almarine, who sends her away while she is pregnant with his child. Granny and the men at the local store consider his behavior necessary, but the fact remains that Emmy has been treated horribly. *Oral History* is intriguing because it simultaneously relies on superstition and mystery as sources of entertainment and yet exposes those elements as tools of oppression. Mothers are the narrative "others" in this novel, particularly when they also are women of color. For every cursed pair of earrings or eerie whistle of the wind in the novel, there is a character like Emmy, or Almarine's unattractive and overlooked stepdaughter Ora Mae, "working [her] knuckles straight down to the bone" (208).

Oral History drew critical praise from highbrow publications as well as from widely popular ones. In *People* magazine, for instance, the novel was chosen as a "Pick" and called a "delightful and entertaining novel." The *Village Voice* was even more effusive in its review: "You could employ all those familiar ringing terms of praise: 'rare,' 'brilliant,' 'unforgettable.' But Lee Smith and *Oral History* make you wish all those phrases were fresh and new, that all those comparisons had never before been made. For this is a novel deserving of unique praise." The positive reception of *Oral History* led to its selection by the Book-of-the-Month Club and to Lee Smith's emergence as an acclaimed writer.

With praise for Smith came comparisons to other authors. In *The New York Times*, Christopher Lehmann-Haupt likened Smith's portrayals of "rural folk" to those written by William Faulkner, Flannery O'Connor, and Eudora Welty. H.H. Campbell, writing in the *Southern Literary Journal*, emphasized Smith's connection to the Brontë sisters, citing similarities in the details and structures of the writers' novels. Campbell gives special attention to parallels between *Oral History* and *Wuthering Heights*. Several of the names in *Oral History* recall characters from Emily Brontë's novel, and both novels feature chronological structures that move from the present into the past and back again. Thematically, Campbell argues, each novel centers upon a woman "caught between an unsatisfying reality (including an unhappy marriage) on the one hand and her strong, unfulfilled dreams and desires on the other" (146). Comparisons such as these astounded Smith, who modestly called a comparison of herself to Faulkner "ridiculous" (Tate 1).

In many ways *Oral History* marked a change in the sort of writing Smith would continue to publish. With the exception of *Fancy Strut*, none of her previous novels had featured the first-person narratives of many different characters. Her work had also never been set in the Appalachian past, where it could be saturated with folk stories and historical resonance. However, in the works that follow *Oral History* Smith frequently wrote about Appalachia in the nineteenth and early twentieth centuries, visiting the past in *Fair and Tender*

Ladies (1988), *The Devil's Dream* (1992), and *On Agate Hill* (2006). The latter two of those novels also employ multiple narrators, and all include perspectives on Appalachia from its residents as well as from outsiders.

Just three years after its 1983 publication, *Oral History* made its theater debut as the play *EarRings*. Adapted from Smith's novel by Don Baker, *Earrings* split the Cantrell family's story into three acts along generational lines. Almarine, Dory, and Pearl and Sally each anchored an act of the play. In a 1988 issue of *Theatre Journal,* William W. French praised the production's "flow of language and sensibility," achieved through the use of folk music interwoven with the actors' voices (421). French also noted that the play's casting added a layer of symbolism to Smith's material. The same actor portrayed Pricey Jane, Dory, and Pearl in the 1988 staging, while another took on the outsider roles of Richard Burlage and Parrot Blankenship, thus suggesting similarities among the characters themselves.

Oral History was also adapted by the magazine *Redbook,* which printed a condensed version of the novel, before its publication, as "The Mystery in the Hills." "It was *terrible*," Smith confessed to Edwin Arnold, "to have [each character] to come and just speak for three sentences" (Tate 16). The *Redbook* version also played up the "Gothic Appalachian" aspect of *Oral History* in an attempt to appeal to what Smith calls the "serious middlebrow" readership. The novel was Smith's third to be adapted by *Redbook,* which paid well for publishing rights and exposed Smith to its broad audience.

Structure and the Past

At the time of its publication, *Oral History* was the most intricately structured novel Smith had written. The book employs a frame narrative, which allows Smith to move the story from the present into the distant past and back again. Within this arrangement several smaller-scale structural choices are also significant. The portion of the story that is set in the past, for instance, is recorded both "orally" and in written form. While Granny Younger's voice is presented as captured on Jennifer's tape, the story from Richard Burlage's point of view is taken from his memoirs, which, according to the novel, were published by a university press. The difference between these sources could hardly be more striking. A typical Granny Younger line reads: "I been here a long time. Years. I know what I know. I know moren most folks and that's a fact" (27). Richard, pretentious and dreamy, writes in a more formal, self-conscious style: "I am torn asunder by conflicting thoughts, each one as valid, it seems to me, as its opposite. I am a sinner, bound for hell; I am a saint, purified by love; I am only a fool" (166). Smith's diverse fictional sources raise issues of authenticity and belief in *Oral History.*

Another structural strategy, exemplified by the juxtaposition of Granny's story with that of Burlage, is Smith's use of characters who are insiders and outsiders in the mountain community encompassing Hoot Owl Holler. While Richard spends only five months in Black Rock, Granny Younger lives there for her whole life. Richard's story reaches locations beyond the Virginia mountains, catching the attention of academics at least as far away as Louisiana. Granny's story, presumably, remains untold to most listeners even after Jennifer records it. Most characters fall neatly into either the insider or outsider category; only a few characters divide their lives between Hoot Owl and other locations. By delivering stories from persons and sources in both the novel's past and its present, Smith creates a fluid historical narrative in which truth is elusive as well as complex.

Oral History opens with the italicized words of a third-person narrator who has access to some of Jennifer's and her estranged grandmother Ora Mae's thoughts. The voice tells how Jennifer too easily classifies her mountain relatives as "so sweet, so simple, so kind" and how Ora Mae finds Jennifer much "like her mother Pearl," a restless woman who left her husband and daughter to embark on a relationship with one of her high school students (16, 20). The voice is also privy to the overwritten notes that Jennifer takes as she interacts with her family, and it breaks from italics to reproduce two pages of them. Jennifer writes that her professor, Dr. Bernie Ripman, "wanted [her] to expand [her] consciousness, [her] tolerance, [her] depth," and wonders how she could "repay him for the new frontiers of self-knowledge [she has] crossed" (19). The pretension with which Jennifer writes suggests that she is allowing preconceptions and unexamined personal goals to cloud her objectivity when it comes to observing her family. Jennifer "sees in the mountain people exactly what her professor has encouraged her to see," the critic Suzanne W. Jones has written, and "to adjust for complexity, she simply omits from her report what does not fit her expectations" (103).

Jennifer writes, for instance, about her "new appreciation for these colorful, interesting folk. My *roots*," but she does not mention that, "close up," her grandfather Luther "smells terrible: body odor, tobacco, something else" (18, 282). Jennifer's assessment of Little Luther shows that she cannot reliably describe or interpret her living family members and casts doubt upon her ability to interpret the dead. Because of her comparative blindness, it is important that Smith follows Jennifer's sections with sections in the voices of such characters as Granny Younger, Jink Cantrell, and even Luther. The novel's middle sections, Jones argues, operate as a "corrective" to Jennifer's narrative, giving readers access to stories that Jennifer would gloss over. As Jones puts it, Jennifer "does not understand how oral history works to relate individuals to a group nor does she see it as the dynamic process that it is—a complex relationship between teller and listener, between events and transmission of events" (104). The transcribed voices of Jennifer's mountain family provide a purer look at this process, drawn as they are from unabridged voices.

However, as Erica Abrams Locklear argues, it is only Smith's actual reading audience that is privy to those transcribed voices. The "fictional reading audience," a group that Locklear singles out, is a group with access to Jennifer's version of her family's history and, presumably, no knowledge of her ancestors' first-person accounts (177). The reading public within the space of the novel also has access to Richard Burlage's memoir, which was published, in the fictional audience's world, by Louisiana State University Press. By limiting the documents and stories to which her fictional audience has access, Smith makes a clear statement about the ways that we, her real audience, consume and distort historical information. "Ultimately," Locklear posits, "Smith creates Oral History . . . as [a counternarrative] that rhetorically works to reshape her reading audience's perceptions of Appalachia, Appalachian women, and literacy" (177). Specifically, the voices of Granny Younger, Jink Cantrell, and Sally provide a counternarrative to the written histories of Jennifer and Richard Burlage, undermining their cultural authority. Still, the novel begins and ends with the words of Jennifer and the nameless narrator closely associated with her. By placing conventional sources of historical information in a bookend position, Smith both questions their authenticity through juxtaposition and provides, as Locklear puts it, "a rhetorical statement about how academic versions of Appalachia always seem to have the first and last word when chronicling the region for readers" (178).

This is not to say that Smith believes, simply by virtue of being first-person and from the past, that a voice should be accepted as correct, authentic, or even honest. In fact, in a 1984 interview Smith expressed doubt that the true history of a person or place could ever really be grasped. "[No] matter how much you do and how much you record people and so on, you never really know exactly the way it was; . . . it is always the teller's tale, that no matter who's telling the story, it is always the teller's tale, and you never finally know exactly the way it was" (Tate 6). But the transcribed vernacular stories in *Oral History* do have a better claim to authenticity, if not veracity, than do the written ones intended for public dissemination, if only because they are offered by the people living in Appalachia rather than by outsiders trying to understand mountain life. The flaws in the Cantrell family's stories and discourse are their own sort of authenticity. This insider-outsider dynamic is one of the most effective that Smith develops in her fiction and also one of the most resonant.

Granny Younger, the first insider to speak in the novel, tells the reader about Almarine's relationships with Red Emmy and Pricey Jane. Granny is disarmingly charming and plainspoken, and her unpretentious mannerisms are convincing, especially because she speaks just after Jennifer. As George Hovis puts it, "Smith places the reader in the position of insider, inviting us—through the charismatic Granny Younger—to suspend our political judgments and cultural biases, as if we too had been reared in the isolation of those mountains" (156). Jocelyn Hazelwood Donlon further clarifies Granny's treatment of the reader, writing that "Granny Younger's use of allusive frames has served to establish us as already a part of the community by the time we realize our position. We are, in effect, what W. Daniel Wilson has termed a 'characterized reader,' one who is embodied in the text and directly addressed by it" (29). Just a few pages into Granny Younger's section of *Oral History*, we have moved from outsiders guided by Jennifer and a voice we do not recognize to part of the mountain community, drawn in by a woman who is both a talker and a healer.

Though Smith makes it easy to trust Granny Younger, critics have pointed out some of the dangers in doing so. One problem, as Paula Gallant Eckard notes, is that Granny Younger is so closely tied to her community that it is problematic to expect her to be objective about it. She writes: "Granny Younger represents the community point of view, and she is the repository of the spiritual life and the collective history of the community" ("The Prismatic Past" 123). Though this representation is positive in many ways, it also raises questions about the accuracy of Granny Younger's narrative, questions only heightened by Granny's frequent condemnation of Red Emmy. Linda Byrd Cook rightly argues that "despite her gender and verbal acumen, [Granny Younger's] collusion with the patriarchy in her judgment and condemnation of Red Emmy is obvious"(63). Entzminger echoes this sentiment when she writes about Granny Younger's unusual degree of autonomy at Hoot Owl, noting how "the healer has power in the community, but mainly because she uses it to aid the patriarchal domestic structure and because she is too old to be considered a sexual being" (162). To maintain her position in the community Granny Younger may well obscure secrets from her own past. "They was a time when me and Isom—but Lord, that's another story," she says at one point, alluding to her relationship with Emmy's father (46). Though we can only speculate about the details of Granny and Isom's relationship, it is possible that Emmy is Granny's daughter, twice abandoned by her mother in the interest of community acceptance.

Similar questions of readerly identification and trust arise in subsequent sections of the novel. Richard Burlage, for instance, who is the first outsider to claim significant space as a speaker in *Oral History,* is an articulate but painfully disconnected teacher who aims to educate mountain children while expanding his own experiential horizons. Burlage possesses some personal traits that make him an appealing narrator for Smith's contemporary readers, most of whom presumably never lived in turn-of-the-century Appalachia. As an outsider Burlage also is new to many of the customs and peculiarities of Hoot Owl. His section was, within the novel's world, published by a university press, which suggests that his writing has been accepted—as his granddaughter Jennifer's will be—as historical evidence by an academic body. However, Burlage's own words should serve as a warning against too fully accepting his conclusions. On the first page of his journal he writes that he expects his sojourn in the mountains to be "a pilgrimage back through time, a pilgrimage to a simpler era, back—dare I hope it—to the very roots of consciousness and belief" (97). Burlage is, from the moment he departs Richmond, disinclined to see mountain residents as his contemporaries or as anything short of elemental figures. As Jones points out, "Smith underlines the problem in Richard's perception by repeatedly having him fail to see Dory's face clearly" (108). While it is relatively easy to see Burlage's shortcomings as an incisive narrator, his section does serve to undermine stereotypes about the residents of Hoot Owl Holler; his writing advances a between-the-lines perspective by way of its obvious blind spots.

Because neither Granny, an orally recorded mountain insider, nor Richard, a writer and outsider, proves a trustworthy historical source, Smith's juxtaposition of their sections suggests the real difficulty in assembling an accurate historical narrative. In *Oral History*'s last long section, however, Smith does offer hope that history can be grappled with honestly and insightfully, even if events cannot be definitively explained or understood. For this purpose she chooses to use the spoken narrative of Sally Wade. Sally's plainspoken but articulate narrative repositions the novel after Burlage's lengthy section; hers is not only the longest section that follows Burlage's; it also is the most grounded. Sally's words manage to seem simultaneously effortless and thoughtful. When she speaks of her mother Dory, for instance, Sally says, "the funny thing about our family at that time was how the whole thing turned around her. It's like the kaleidoscope we got that year for Christmas, . . . how it had a bright blue spot in the middle of all the patterns" (238). In a single remembrance Sally combines an actual, simple event from her childhood with a rather complex idea about her mother's central role in the family's life. That Sally is a verbal artist without much trace of artifice makes her an appealing narrator. A contemporary woman, Sally has a language and a lifestyle that should also be more familiar to the novel's readers than those of her ancestors. Although Sally writes from a familiar present, her story is still an important and weighty one; Eckard notes how "Sally's narrative is equal in length to Granny Younger's, bringing the novel full circle" (127).

That Sally's adult life is both less tumultuous and less exciting than the lives of her ancestors is reflective of Smith's thoughts about the changing spatial landscape of her Virginia mountains. "Once life is homogeneous," Smith has said, "once it gets all pasteurized and evened out and everything, . . . the grandeur isn't nearly as possible" (Tate 8). As the daughter of Dory Cantrell and Luther Wade, Sally is endowed with both her mother's sensuality and her father's lyricism. However, the earthy, plainspoken way that Sally describes her sex life with Roy contrasts starkly with Burlage's descriptions of his relationship with Sally's mother. While Dory and Richard had clandestine and consuming sex in the local schoolhouse, Sally and Roy "fool around" in bed with his leg propped up and in a cast. Sally's easy sensuality makes her happy, whereas Dory's is ultimately destructive. In a similar way Sally's lyricism also expresses itself in a more everyday way than does Little Luther's. While her father expresses his in song and music, Sally uses hers for conversation. She is, as Cook has written, also a prolific talker; she is "filled with words and shares all of them with her husband" (83). Thus the Cantrell family traits manifest in safer, more stable ways in Sally than in her ancestors; while this manifestation is not true for all the Cantrell/Wade children of her generation, it does suggest that the contemporary mountains are a tamer place, where love affairs and curses play out on a smaller scale.

There are other voices at work in *Oral History,* most of them belonging to residents of Hoot Owl Holler. Rose Hibbits and Jink Cantrell each narrate a section, as does Mrs. Luddie Davenport, an old woman in the community who believes that Red Emmy haunts the Cantrell home place. These sections ground the longer ones by suggesting the degree to which the Cantrells' tumultuous history is truly a community experience, something that affects and interests their neighbors and others not directly involved. The inclusion of these shorter, sometimes peripheral sections also magnifies Smith's decision not to include sections voiced by the likes of Red Emmy and Dory, neither of whom serves as a narrator in the novel despite being so central to its conceits. Though Smith originally drafted a section from Red Emmy's perspective—it sounded, she said, like "bad Benjy" of *The Sound and the Fury*—her editor advised her to excise it, thus leaving Emmy as "an unexplained mystery at [the book's] core" (Tate 17). Margaret D. Bauer argues that voicelessness is an appropriate narrative condition for other central characters, too: "Giving to these transcendental characters actual voices would declare their physical reality and thereby diminish their legendary stature" ("No Mere Endurance" 25).

Collectively, the juxtaposition of Smith's omissions and inclusions paints more than just Red Emmy as an "unexplained mystery." The past of the novel, from witches to romance and parentage, is ultimately indecipherable, a reality that Smith deliberately cultivated. In an interview Smith admitted, "I think that was one thing I was trying to say in *Oral History*. It's just the idea that you never know what happened in the past, really. . . . When you go back to look for it, all you ever get is your interpretation of it. No matter how much you do and how much you record people and so on, you never really know exactly the way it was; . . . it is always the teller's tale, that no matter who's telling the story, it is always the teller's tale, and you never finally know exactly the way it was." (Tate 6)

While it acknowledges that certainty is elusive, *Oral History* remains an invitation to pay attention to history: the cobbled-together narrative created over a century by different storytellers is more accurate than any of their individual tales. An event or perception's survival in family legend does not guarantee its literal truth, but its associations and the reactions it inspires are, in their own ways, revelatory.

In an addendum to the 2003 paperback edition of *Oral History*, Smith noted that the novel's structure, with its frame, unreliable narrators, and written and oral perspectives, proved confusing to some readers. "Red Emmy and Almarine and Dory and Pearl and Sally and all those stories," she explains, "were on the tape that Jennifer took back to her class. . . . I'm afraid nobody got it." A likely source of this confusion is the novel's final section, which explains what happens when Jennifer presents her ancestral research to Dr. Ripman and her college classmates. "Jennifer's tape," according to this section, "will have enough banging and crashing and wild laughter on it to satisfy even the most hardened cynic in the class" (284). Though the tape did record noises in the house, there is no mention of voices or long stories on its reels; only the conventional sounds of an old and haunted house. There is, in fact, no indication whether Jennifer herself has heard the voices of her family's past. If she has, it seems unlikely that she would be able to dismiss her relatives, as the omniscient narrator says she does, as simply "very primitive people, resembling nothing so much as some sort of early tribe" (285). Though we cannot know for certain how many, if any, of the stories Jennifer has heard, it is clear that she remains a true outsider to her mountain clan, unable to accept or even access her family's complex and often painful lives.

Myth and Religion

Because *Oral History* tells of four generations in the Cantrell family, it covers a larger span of years than did Smith's earlier novels. The novel, while rarely didactic, thus charts some of the changes in Appalachia and its residents as the twentieth century progresses. Smith addresses these changes through both literal details in the story—Pricey Jane's magazines, for instance, and Al Cantrell's shag-carpeted van—and metaphorical motifs, some of which run through the entire novel. One of the subtle ways in which Smith comments on the evolution of Hoot Owl Holler, specifically, is by her use of spiritual imagery. In Granny Younger's section of the novel, which is the first on Jennifer's tape, there is little mention of church, Jesus, or other signifiers of Christianity. Instead, there are pointed and frequent references to ancient mythologies and goddesses. By the novel's midpoint, though, the Christian churches near Hoot Owl are central, drawing the attention of Richard Burlage as he pursues Dory Cantrell. The church scenes in this section are powerful, but they do not possess the sense of mystery and ethereal possibility that colors Granny Younger's stories. The spirituality of Appalachia, Smith suggests, is becoming less steeped in the natural world and mysticism and more in the relatively restrained environment of Christianity. This change is even more marked in Sally Cantrell's section of the novel, which is conspicuously grounded and matter-of-fact: mystery and danger have, to an extent, been tamed by livelihoods that seem more stable but also more mundane. Thus, spiritual motifs in *Oral History* serve as both culturally significant details in their own right and signifiers of broader change in Appalachia.

A large share of critical attention has been given to the spiritual elements present in Granny Younger's section of the novel, which range from symbolically loaded character names to iconography and referential situations. In *Lee Smith*, for instance, Dorothy Combs Hill devotes most of her chapter on *Oral History* to drawing connections between character names and mythic characters and conventions. She classifies Almarine as a sort of water god and rightly notes that even Granny Younger's rather plain name evokes ethereal ideas through its juxtaposition of old and young. "A reversal of full cycle," Hill writes, "[Granny Younger's] name implies eternal return" (58). Cook makes similar associations when she points out the importance of Red Emmy's rumored home, which is a cave. The cave, Cook suggests, implies Emmy's "sacred nature" because of its associations with mythical origin stories. Emmy is, in fact, the character most undeniably painted as mythic. Mysterious in her own right, she is also described as a sort of sun goddess, with "reddest red [hair], a red so dark it was nigh to purple" and "color flamed out in her cheeks" (44). According to Granny Younger, Emmy vanishes at will from Almarine's sight and uses a wish-granting redbird to lead Almarine to her bathing pool. However, part of Emmy's mystery derives from the difficulty of tying her to any one mythic character, or even to any single tradition of storytelling. As Bauer has written, Emmy is as much a "wicked witch" as a goddess, "hovering in the margins" of Almarine and Pricey Jane's "fairytale" ("No Mere Endurance" 24). The variety of mythologies and stories with which Emmy and the other characters mentioned by Granny Younger intensifies the sense of wildness and possibility in her section of *Oral History*.

Though Granny Younger's story does not often reference churchgoing or Jesus, the spiritual motifs she includes do occasionally mix Christian symbolism with their references to ancient mythology and other legends and traditions. Conrad Ostwalt, for instance, has noted that "Granny Younger typifies the confusion of superstition with traditional Christianity by reciting a magical formula to stop bleeding. The formula is based on Ezekiel 16:6 . . . but in Lee Smith's mystical, sacred Appalachian setting, it takes on magical and supernatural qualities" (108).

Entzminger points out instances of overlap in *The Belle Gone Bad*, explaining how, for instance, even Red Emmy has Christian associations with Lilith, a figure of Hebrew legend. Lilith was Adam's original counterpart but refused to recognize his authority, behavior that led to her banishment and subsequent attempts to endanger Adam's children. This narrative parallels Emmy's story, as community members blame her for the misfortune that befalls the Cantrell family after Almarine ousts her, pregnant, from his land. Almarine has chosen, as Bauer writes, "to stay in Eden without Eve rather than lose Eden, which is what he fears will happen, for his sexual relations with Red Emmy leave him too exhausted to work his land" ("No Mere Endurance" 23). Bauer touches here on two examples of how religious motifs are extrapolated throughout *Oral History*. The first is how love of land is itself a sort of mountain spirituality; the second, how Emmy, a beguiling and spiritualized woman, is demonized by the Hoot Owl community when she interferes with male authority. These two are not unrelated.

The spiritual importance of land in *Oral History* is one of the elements that most directly ties the novel to the Southern literary canon. Bauer specifically draws a parallel between the valuation and exploitation of land in Smith's novel and in Faulkner's *The Sound and the Fury,* citing the symbolic similarity of "Ghostland," the theme park built around the old Cantrell cabin, to the golf course built on Compson family land. Both pieces of land are sites of spiritual and emotional investment that are repurposed for commercial enterprises, ones that cash in on elements of the land's actual history. In Faulkner the golf course offers middle-class men an artificial approximation of a privileged man's life of leisure, on land that was once his. In the case of Hoot Owl Holler the land's dark history is diminished for the financial benefit of the Cantrell descendants. The change in the land's valuation is highlighted by the fact that Almarine's "grandson", Al, is the person who oversees its conversion to Ghostland. The child of Ora Mae and Little Luther Wade, Al shares common family members with Almarine but is not biologically descended from him. While the first Almarine values his land to a fault—making it, as Hovis has written, a stand-in for the family ties he lacked—his grandson sees the land as a means to a financial end. Al, Bauer observes, "is more concerned with the value of the land he lives on than with the humanity of the characters in these legends, which he is violating through exploitation" ("No Mere Endurance" 37). From Almarine to Al, Hoot Owl Holler has come to carry and signify generations of memories and tragedies, but even those have their price in contemporary Appalachia.

The spiritual connection between people and their land is not a vague or undefined connection in *Oral History*. Ostwalt has written at length about how the connection represents a sort of dual-spiritual aesthetic at work in Lee Smith's mountains. He argues that the first spiritual impulse "appears in the form of traditional religions that attempt to transcend the mountain peaks and valley floors; the second is characterized by an elemental, supernatural power bound up by nature and the mountains themselves" (98). Though these spiritual forces coexist, the Cantrell family's narrative suggests that the elemental, nature-tied spirituality ceded ground to traditional religions in the twentieth century, in terms of adherence if not intrinsic power. Ostwalt astutely describes some of the implications that Smith's attention to changed spirituality in Appalachia carries: "The connection to the elemental, which depends on the connection to nature, the land, the spiritual, and the mythic past, becomes tenuous as the unspoiled, wild beauty of the land that captivated such characters as Almarine Cantrell and Richard Burlage slowly yields to strip mines, shopping malls, and towns and villages. As concrete and pavement fill the mountain hollows, the witches disappear, superstition is replaced by religion, and Smith's female characters, who had enjoyed a mystical connection with the primal, search with fewer results for that secret power available through nature and spirit" (110).

Ostwalt's passage connects Almarine's relationship to spirituality to his relationship with Red Emmy, one of those mountain women in possession of "secret power" and a "mystical connection with the primal." Although Emmy seems powerful largely because of the mythic way Granny Younger describes her, she does have traits that support those descriptions. Emmy is unusually tall for a woman, and she also works Almarine's land instead of doing the household chores which mountain women commonly were assigned. Yet, as Almarine's wild and consuming love for her yields to community pressure to reject her, Emmy violently loses any agency she may have had in the Hoot Owl environs. Her initial expulsion from the community and Almarine leads to rumored murder; Granny Younger suggests that Almarine finds and kills her after the deaths of Pricey Jane and his child. In seeking to assert his independence from her, Almarine submits himself to the organized patriarchal community that seeks to disempower Emmy. These are the men—and Granny Younger—at Joe Johnson's store, with whom Almarine plays cards and drinks before and after his time with Emmy. Threatened by Almarine and Emmy's frequent lovemaking—it is uncommon and keeps him from their store—and by Emmy's near-equality with her lover, Granny Younger brands her a witch and seeks to oust her and restore order. Like the natural spirituality with which she is associated, Emmy is rejected in favor of a patriarchal belief system; she becomes the scapegoat for the curse that seems to plague the Cantrell descendants. Entzminger gets to the center of this plot point when she argues that the curse "does not come from Emmy's witchcraft but from a community that sentences its women to lives of constrained passivity and rejects those who resist conformity" (163). Thus religion, land, female power, and sexuality are all fused in the story of Almarine and Emmy, and to a lesser extent later in *Oral History*.

Byrd addresses those later sections in her work on myth, religion, and sexuality. Writing particularly about the relationship between Richard Burlage and Dory Cantrell, she notes that "Richard finds in Dory the divinity for which he has long been searching. His flirtation with the rural church of Tug runs parallel to his relationship with Dory . . . because Dory and Richard come together right after a revival" (134). Although this coupling makes for a spiritually significant start, Cook correctly observes that living in the myth becomes a problem, albeit one that is worse for the female in the relationship. The ethereal relationship cannot last long under the assault of reality, especially with the irresolute Richard as its steward. What is, for Richard, a beautiful memory, enriching experience, and sweet loss is destruction for Dory. She is the one with children to bear and raise, and she has fewer options than does Richard for finding happiness elsewhere. In her story Dory unites the abstract spiritual with the jarringly grounded, preparing the way through her sad narrative for the Cantrells who follow. The same train that brings her Richard Burlage and an exciting love story later causes her death as she lays on its track. Dory is mythic, but she is also heartbreakingly human.

Mothers and Others

Mothers in *Oral History* are frequently absent from the lives of their children, but they are also central to the novel's plots and deeply resonant for many of its characters. Beginning in the cave of Red Emmy, who lives alone with her father Isom, Smith chronicles homes that are largely bereft of matriarchs. Where mothers are absent, other maternal figures sometimes take their places; Dory, for instance, is largely responsible for her siblings after the death of her mother Pricey Jane until her aunt Vashti arrives to run the household. Vashti and her daughter Ora Mae ultimately raise many of the Cantrell children, stepping into the maternal roles vacated by Dory and Pearl. Although Vashti and Ora Mae are important characters for reasons other than their mixed-race heritage, the women both represent racial others in the novel, which is especially significant because Hoot Owl Holler has been such a racially homogenous society. As Katerina Prajznerová has written, Vashti and Ora Mae are a "conspicuous embodiment of the intermarriage and exchange between Native Americans and American Europeans in Smith's Appalachian fiction" (65). Prajznerová notes the ways in which Vashti, particularly, is associated with Cherokee elements and motifs. In *Oral History* motherhood is linked with difference through Vashti and Ora Mae.

From a literal standpoint the attention Smith gives to mothers and their work in the novel is instructive. In Pricey Jane's brief section of the novel, for instance, the amount of time she spends working while also frequently nursing her child suggests the intense work to which a typical twentieth-century Appalachian mother may have committed herself. Pricey Jane "sends Eli around with a panful of dried corn to scatter while she sets Dory up on a pallet in the floor and makes some cornbread and cuts some sidemeat off the piece of it hanging there by the chimney and fries it. She nurses Dory again" (72). Vashti, too, is depicted as a hard worker, "making coffee and frying eggs" within hours of arriving at Almarine's cabin, and Ora Mae raises both Dory and, for a while, Dory's children (86). Like Toni Morrison and Ellen Douglas, among others, Smith treats the domestic work of women and children as a worthy subject of her art.

Mothers in *Oral History* are scarce and also difficult for other characters to understand. Sometimes this enigma exists because of unexplained physical absence; Red Emmy's mother, for instance, is probably never heard from, and Emmy herself physically vanishes from the Cantrells' lives after she reportedly becomes pregnant with a child of her own. In part, too, this scarcity of mothers reflects historical reality. According to the U.S. census, a person born in 1870 could expect to live for approximately forty years; by the turn of the century, life expectancy hovered around age fifty, and it is possible that these ages would be lower in Appalachia than in the rest of the country. However, most of the mothers in Smith's novel do not die simply because they have reached a relatively old age. Poisoned milk, possible suicide, and complications of childbirth kill Pricey Jane, Dory, and Pearl, respectively, leaving their children motherless. These dark deaths are attributed to Red Emmy's curse, a community scapegoat that allows men and women to continue positioning Emmy as a villain.

Specifically, Smith's mothers often suffer because of Hoot Owl society's inability to reconcile their embodiment of both the sexual and the maternal, despite their necessary inextricability. This fear of the sexual is particularly evident in the stories of Emmy and Dory, but even mothers almost entirely absent from the novel are drawn into this fear. Pricey Jane, for instance, recalls how "if you asked her [mother] about love . . . she'd act like there was something shameful in it" (68). As Byrd has written, "to all these women, the union of sexuality and motherhood is natural, but to most of society, maternity is the end-product rather than the site of sexuality" (141). That Emmy and Almarine continue their frequent lovemaking even after she is rumored to be pregnant is the reason she is finally expelled. Hovis points out that "Granny is disturbed not so much by Emmy's sexuality as by the fact that she is openly sexual at the same time that she desires to be domestic" (149). Similarly, Richard leaves Dory behind soon after they conceive twins. That Richard does not realize she is pregnant is immaterial; the significant point is that he cannot see a wild and sensual mountain woman as an appropriate wife and mother in his Richmond life.

Male characters, though, are not the only ones who cannot reconcile sex and motherhood. Dory's daughter Pearl, who is a product of her relationship with Richard Burlage, abandons her family for an adventurous, illegal liaison with a high school student, seeking sexual fulfillment from a man with whom she has no children. The character of Pearl echoes the Queen in *The Last Day the Dogbushes Bloomed,* though her choice of a younger sexual partner makes her actions even more scandalous. In *Oral History* it is only in Sally's second marriage, to Roy, that the maternal and the sexual are successfully reconciled, and even that linkage is conditional. Though Sally and Roy have a fulfilling sex life and enjoy spending time as a family with her grandchildren, they did not have or raise children together as a couple.

Still, critics frequently assert that Sally and Roy's relationship represents successful reconciliation of the sexual woman and the maternal, familial lifestyle. Cook, for one, has written that "healing is suggested by Sally and Roy's marriage, one based on equality and communication" (83). Sally's words are, in large part, what sets her apart from Red Emmy and Dory, neither of whom narrates the novel or is shown talking much with their lovers. Sally loves to talk and Roy loves to listen, even during their lovemaking. That Roy listens seems to be key; it is his behavior, rather than Sally's loquacity, that is necessary for their happy union. Sally's first marriage helps us see the importance of Roy's listening skills. Though Sally liked to talk to her first husband, too, he "didn't believe in talking to women and he never said one word; . . . [he would] just roll over and go to sleep" (234). Hovis sees this as commentary by Smith on a male partner's responsibility in his relationship: "Roy is the kind of a man Smith seems to be calling for, someone who can accept a woman as both sexual and a source of wisdom, not one or the other" (161). Wisdom is, of course, tied to responsibility and motherhood. Through Sally, Byrd argues, "Smith insists on the survival and even proliferation of the sexual mother" (142).

Though the plights of these female characters are themselves significant, they also are suggestive of larger ideas. For example, Eckard has noted that, "while these women are given little voice themselves, the voices Smith creates to tell their stories reflect the plural realities and multiple modes of expression associated with female subjectivity" (*Maternal* 140). Smith thus underscores the uncertainty of the history that her narrative strategies suggest by placing voiceless mothers at the center of it. Eckard goes on to say that, "sadly, the maternal in *Oral History* also functions as a metaphor for the fragile culture of the mountains, soon to be overwhelmed, displaced, and silenced by larger social forces from the outside world" (138). Mothers are, in this approximation, akin to "others," narrative signifiers of difference and, often, of exploitation. While this is a secondary position for some characters—Dory is first a mother, which puts her in the position of "other"—*Oral History* also devotes narrative space to characters who are inherently mother and other. The most conspicuous embodiment of both roles is Vashti, who, along with her daughter Ora Mae, is of an indeterminate race. Vashti "looks like she might be part Indian" according to Almarine's neighbor and admirer Rose Hibbits: "She is a tall woman with thick shiny black hair, dark complected, of course, and a big strong nose and a wide mouth and big dark eyes" (86). In a 2001 interview with Prajznervoá, Smith confirms her intention that Vashti and Ora Mae be read as Native Americans. "I've always been really fascinated with . . . this sense of the other. . . . I was just always so curious about Melungeons or about Indians or about people that lived way, way up in the hills" (109).

Vashti and Ora Mae have been others in an extratextual sense, as well; in secondary criticism Prajznerová is one of few critics to emphasize their role in *Oral History*. As in the novel itself, the women have taken subordinate positions to Red Emmy, Dory, and Sally Wade. On one hand, this relative obscurity makes a great deal of sense. While Emmy and Dory are sources of fascination, longing, and sometimes anger or envy for multiple characters, Ora Mae and Vashti do not often inspire emotional reactions from other characters. Because of their chronologies and relative seclusion at the Cantrell home place, too, they are barely glimpsed by either Granny Younger or Richard Burlage, whose perspectives dictate much of the novel's content. Still, when analyzing a work so invested in telling untold stories and questioning dominant historical narratives, it seems remiss to avoid examining the resonance of its most othered

characters. Prajznerová points out multiple instances in which she believes critics have misread scenes involving Vashti and Ora Mae. With respect to Vashti,
the critic argues that when the character has received critical attention, it has
been as an "embodiment of dependent and circumscribed female domesticity"
(77). Citing statements by Anne Goodwyn Jones and Linda Byrd Cook, among
others, Prajznerová suggests that critics have too easily dismissed Vashti and
Almarine's relationship as either "loveless" or characterized by "loneliness and
isolation" (78). Instead, Prajznerová contends, "Vashti's efficient running of the
household does not need to imply her unhappy confinement and patriarchal
subjugation . . . . She searches Almarine out because of her sense of family ties"
rather than her need for a man to care for her and Ora Mae (79). (As suggested
by Emmy's troubles, "need" for a woman such as Vashti could apply to male
protection from the community rather than to help running a household.)

Though Prajznerová's critical angle is compelling, she does not provide
persuasive textual support for the existence of a loving familial relationship
between Vashti and Almarine. Still, she does expose some overstatement by
the critics she quotes, and her admonition that Vashti has not been adequately
accounted for is just. Prajznerová questions, for instance, Dorothy Combs
Hill's assertion that Vashti's story marks "the elimination of the wife of will,
the one who will not show off her body when the patriarch bids, and the sub-
stitution of the obedient Esther" (72). Though Hill draws this analysis from her
reading of the biblical Vashti's story, it is at odds with what we know of *Oral
History*'s Vashti. To paint Vashti, whom the text depicts as a strong and imposing woman capable of quickly taking over a household, as a figure of weakness
and subjugation is to stray too far from the details of the novel. Indeed, even
when she is physically weak and on her deathbed, Vashti "has to have a glass
of water right there on the night table just so, if you put it on the wrong side
she'll yell and you have to get up and go move it" (216).

Although, like Red Emmy before her, Vashti is a figure whose early life is
mysterious, Smith reveals glimpses of her life at Hoot Owl Holler through Jink
Cantrell, her son with Almarine. One of the couple's five biological children,
Jink reads as intelligent—he impresses Richard Burlage in the classroom—and
reliable, with no apparent motive to misrepresent his family. In the few pages
he narrates Jink recounts how "Mamaw locked me down in the root cellar for
lying" for two days, and observes Vashti "working along with the men [like]
she always does" (189, 192). Later he recalls how Dory "wouldn't do a thing
Mamaw said, which tickled me and Mary, but Mamaw liked to rode her to
death, telling her what was good for her" while she was pregnant (193). Vashti,
then, is a hard worker who, like Red Emmy, does not resign herself to traditional

women's chores. She is also a strict disciplinarian and stepmother to a beautiful girl who will not listen to her. It is this last, circumstantial trait that is perhaps most useful in constructing an alternate reading of Vashti. As Ora Mae will do after her, she persists in trying to mold the Cantrell offspring: she tells them what is best for them, despite their reluctance to listen. Though Jink's narration makes it reasonably clear that Vashti is not a gentle or soothing parent, she seems to have the best interests of her children, biological or not, in mind.

The dynamic between Vashti and Dory makes sense in the context of a discussion between Smith and Prajnerová: "[Vashti] and Ora Mae had that sort of sense of the future, some sort of knowing more than they wanted to know, some sort of life force that they had" (109). Collectively, Vashti's actions and Smith's statement suggest that Vashti sees herself as a sort of protector, loving or not, of the Cantrell children, meant to strengthen and prepare them for the hardships she sees in their futures. Perhaps because of the trouble she can sense, Vashti is dismissive of people like Little Luther Wade, to whom she "wouldn't give . . . much credit" and accuses of having his "'head in the clouds'" (195). That Luther will eventually marry Dory Cantrell is something that Vashti can foresee, as is the tragedy that will follow their marriage when Dory is killed by a train. Of course, while some of Vashti's traits are made reasonably clear in the novel, her exact motivations remain opaque; hers is not one of the voices on Jennifer's tape recorder.

Though Vashti does not have a section in the novel, her daughter Ora Mae voices her thoughts in a short section of *Oral History*. Almost immediately, she addresses her ability to foresee the future. "I wisht I didn't know what-all I know, nor have to do what-all I have to. . . . I've been working my knuckles straight down to the bone taking care of Cantrells" (200). These sentiments repeat themselves many times in the few pages Ora Mae claims; she says later "I know what I know but wisht I didn't, I've got the gift you don't never want to have" and "I knowed what I knowed, and I knowed what I had to do" (208). Ora Mae is always "knowing," and in her resentful determination to take care of Cantrells, she often reads as a character shaped by her sense of duty. This force is particularly true in the section where Ora Mae tells the story of her refusal to run away with Parrot Blankenship, whom she loved deeply but "knew" would leave her before long. Still, Ora Mae, like Vashti, is not passive. She is, after all, the woman who chooses not to give Dory the note from Richard Burlage, possibly preventing their long-term union through her choice. Ora Mae also throws Pricey Jane's golden earrings, which she believes carry the family's curse, down from a mountaintop. Sally's description of the moment when she does this is riveting:

She pulled something little out of the pocket, pulled it out slow and painful, the way she does everything, and then she let out the awfulest low sad wail I ever heard. It did not sound like a person at all. It sounded like something right out of the burying ground, some rising up of age and pain. She fiddled with what she had—I'd guessed what it was, by then, and I'll bet you have too—and she got one of them in each hand and held them up, I watched her, for a long, long moment, to her own ears. That old, old ugly woman! It was just about the worst and saddest thing I ever saw. And I've seen some things. Then she slung both arms straight out and threw the earrings into the swirling clouds in the gorge and they went down, down, I guess, to the river so far below, and I guess that's where they are now, thank God. Gone. Ora Mae had the right idea. But she stood there with her arms flung out, like a statue in a church or something, for the longest time. She gave me the creeps. Then she lowered her arms real slow, and while I watched, she shrank back from whatever she was to old Ora Mae again, so old she can't even drive. (277)

In the moment Sally describes, Ora Mae claims her power in a revealing and transformative way. That she holds the earrings to her own ears before flinging them down suggests the complexity of her feelings about the Cantrell family. Although most of her direct comments about the family refer to their dependence on her and their weakness, the gesture she performs with the earrings implies that she, too, has had a longing to wear them, cursed as they may be. The existence of this desire is reinforced in Ora Mae's section, in which she refuses to listen to Rhoda Hibbits when Rhoda tells her that she is a pretty girl. "That was a lie," Ora Mae says; "Dory was the pretty girl" (210).

By doing away with the earrings Ora Mae is not washing her hands of the Cantrells. For years after she flings the jewelry into the gorge, she remains a part of the Cantrell household, marrying Luther Wade and living with Al, his wife Debra, and their children. What she seems to be doing instead is refusing to be consumed with longing and resentment any longer. When Jennifer comes to visit her family, Ora Mae is knitting on the porch, but she is not looking at her needlework. Instead, "she's looking off to the side yard where two of her grandsons, Al's children, have tied string on some june bugs they are swinging around and around through the hot evening air" (13). With Dory's death and Ora Mae's marriage to Luther, Ora Mae finally has become an insider in the Cantrell family; she is, in her big green chair, a matriarchal figure. That she and Luther conceive a son and call him Almarine underscores her thorough absorption into the family.

Oral History closes with a brief matter-of-fact look at what Ora Mae and many of the other characters do after Jennifer leaves Hoot Owl Holler. This look is long-term, revealing, for example, that Jennifer marries her college professor and never returns to her family's ancestral home, that Little Luther and Ora Mae will simply "get sick one by one and then die," and that the theme park Ghostland will charge visitors $4.50 each to listen to eerie laughter and see an empty rocking chair rock (285). As Rosalind B. Reilly has written, "all these details have the disappointing feel of the wide-awake world after an especially powerful dream" (92). This is the price, Reilly argues, of "freedom from illusion." The painful crimes of passion and tragic love stories from the days of Almarine and Dory Cantrell may be laid to rest, but a less enchanting present has taken their place.

CHAPTER 4

Our Years as a Tale That Is Told

Fair and Tender Ladies

In Lee Smith's first four novels her protagonists are young girls and women with artistic temperaments. While Susan Tobey experiments with writing poetry in *The Last Day the Dogbushes Bloomed* and Crystal Spangler takes up crafting in *Black Mountain Breakdown,* neither character is defined by her particular talent. Smith introduces a more committed artist in the novel *Family Linen* (1985). Candy Snipes, a rural beautician, has an integrated personality according to which her art defines her life. Like the artists in many of Smith's short stories—Florrie of "Cakewalk," Cheryl of "Bob, a Dog"—Candy's art is considered humble. Caring and down-to-earth, she beautifies her female clients. In *Fair and Tender Ladies* (1988), however, Smith introduces an integrated artist of a more conventional sort: Ivy Rowe is a writer, through and through. Though she mostly writes letters and never is published, Ivy is the first protagonist in Smith's fiction to make her talent for writing the center of her life. Unlike Candy's work, however, Ivy's art mostly remains personal. She initially dreams of being a famous writer but dedicates herself to caring for her large family instead.

Ivy's talent gives Smith new parameters for her experimentations with voice. *Fair and Tender Ladies* is Smith's first epistolary novel, and it is narrated entirely through Ivy's letters. Beginning at age twelve and continuing until she is near death in her late seventies, Ivy writes letters that tell the story of a life largely spent in one place. She writes to teachers, friends, family members, and even a would-be pen pal, all from the mountains of western Virginia. The audience for Ivy's letters is almost entirely female. In addition to her physical mountain community, which frequently denies her support, Ivy creates a sustaining, though far-flung, community of women through her letters. As Linda Wagner-Martin has argued, Ivy's tapestry of letters is "the thread she follows through—and clear of—the labyrinth of her life of poverty and confusion and femaleness" (28). It does not matter to Ivy that her letters often go unanswered. In fact, many of Ivy's most revealing missives are addressed to her sister Silvaney, whom Ivy knows is dead. "I had to write this letter to you, Silvaney," she writes in one, "to set it all down. I am still in pain and sorrow, but I remain, Your sister, Ivy Rowe" (240). Ivy, Katherine Kearns observes, "orders, clarifies, and makes real the discrete elements of her world" as she reminds herself of her connections and communities in her letters (188).

Ivy is a thoughtful and analytical writer and thus a capable guide through the events of her life. Because so many of Ivy's letters remain unsent, addressed to dead or departed family members who will never read them, she is frank and truthful. In her letters to Silvaney, in particular, Ivy writes with little filter and with almost no regard for her privacy, sharing the sorts of details that would usually become the stuff of diaries or personal journals. As in *Oral History,* Smith creates here intratextual and real-world reading audiences for Ivy's writing. The events of Ivy's life are one part of her story, subject to analysis by Smith's own readers. However, in the letters that Ivy actually mails, Ivy's own analysis provides a second narrative, adding depth and feeling to Smith's novel. Ivy is a reliable narrator, but that does not mean that she is an objective one.

Through Ivy's letters, Smith continues to explore themes prominent in her earlier fiction. The female artist's quest to forge her identity, the history of rural Appalachia, the tension between religion and spirituality, and the importance of storytelling all are focal points of Ivy's letters. In *Fair and Tender Ladies,* though, Smith addresses these themes with a greater sense of optimism and possibility. This sense is most obvious in relation to identity and literacy. While Susan Tobey and Brooke Kinkaid, for instance, struggle to speak their community's discourse or produce an alternative dialogue, Ivy absorbs her community's stories and thrives on writing her own, creating a stable sense of herself in the process. Her writing also becomes, to a large extent, a habit by which her peers identify her; it sets her apart in her rural mountain community, but it also unites her public and private selves. Ivy's integration proves essential for her survival. She feels "starved" when she goes without hearing stories and depressed when she goes without telling them (226).

Ivy's identity also is built upon her dedication to Sugar Fork, where she lives for most of her life. She feels physically connected to the land—"a big yellow sycamore leaf" landing on her porch is "like a blow to [her] heart"—and emotionally invested in protecting it from companies who would cut its lumber and mine its coal (274). Ivy's relationship to her home is inextricably linked to her gender. She does not venture to certain parts of the nearby mountains because she is a girl: "I could of climbed up here by myself, anytime," she thinks, after hiking to the top of Blue Star Mountain with a lover. "But I had not; . . . they said, That is for boys" (233). Just as Ivy feels restricted from areas within her community, she feels incapable of venturing far beyond expected boundaries. An unexpected pregnancy prevents her from leaving for Boston as a young woman, and her familial responsibilities yoke her to Sugar Fork later. Home, for Ivy, is a space deeply characterized by her gender and her family, for both good and bad.

Ivy's reverence for the land is so intense as to be spiritual. Though she never feels an intense connection to the Christianity to which members of her family and community subscribe, she is a seeker of natural beauty. "I would just as soon sit in the breezeway looking out at Bethel Mountain," Ivy writes, "as to go to church" (206). Ivy especially turns to the land when she is grieving. After her husband Oakley's death, for instance, Ivy writes that "some days I feel old as the hills themselves which I walk among now almost without ceasing" (274). She is physically and emotionally of the mountains, despite the attempts of many people—men, especially—to convert her to a more conventional religion. Since publishing *Fair and Tender Ladies* Smith has continually fictionalized the tension between patriarchal religious traditions and potentially woman-centered nature-based spirituality.

Ivy's relative strength is reflected in her writing style. Though she records plenty of hardship and pain in her letters, Ivy does so with such lively writing and self-awareness that her story is a beautiful one; without careful reading it is easy to become caught up in Ivy's artistry and gloss over her considerable struggles. Unlike Crystal Spangler in *Black Mountain Breakdown* or Pearl from *Oral History*, Ivy, as Dorothy Combs Hill has written, "embodies female victory over the social forces, externally inflicted and internally realized, that would destroy her" (109). Thus the introduction of Ivy marks a dramatic turning point in Lee Smith's female characters. By creating Ivy, Kearns argues, "Smith bespeaks her own growing confidence in the mutually regenerative powers of life and art" (191). Ivy is preceded in Smith's fiction by women who strive to assimilate and fill conventional roles in their southern communities. She is followed, though, by Katie Cocker, by Mary Copeland, and by Molly Petree, women who triumph, in ways both subtle and enormous, over pain and the limitations their societies place on women. Molly, the sometime-narrator and protagonist of *On Agate Hill* (2006), is Ivy's most direct descendant: like Ivy, she writes from her girlhood until her death, chronicling her refusal to accept a woman's traditional role and her pursuit of passion in difficult circumstances.

Smith drew on multiple women as sources of inspiration in crafting her seventh novel. She chose, for instance, to write *Fair and Tender Ladies* as an epistolary novel largely because of a packet of letters she purchased at a Greensboro, North Carolina, flea market. "I got real interested in the idea of somebody's letters being a sort of work of art," she said in a 1989 interview. "You know, letters over their whole lifetime" (Tate 62). Smith also was inspired by her encounter with Lou Crabtree, an unassuming older woman who brought to Smith's writing class "a suitcase full of this stuff that she'd been writing and writing and writing." Crabtree's lifetime of writing without seeking publication led Smith to think about writing as a process and about the ways women's art often is unrecognized in the public sphere. More personally, Smith was influenced by the illness and death of her mother, Gig. "With Ivy Rowe," she said, "I really needed to be making up somebody who could just take whatever 'shit hit the fan.' Sort of assimilate it and go on." Calling Ivy a "role model," Smith imbued her narrator with strengths she coveted while handling her mother's death and difficulties with her teenaged sons (Tate 65).

Ivy Rowe proved popular with both critics and Smith's readership. Writing in the *New York Times Book Review*, W. P. Kinsella called *Fair and Tender Ladies* Smith's "most ambitious and most fully realized novel to date," claiming readers "will be sorry when this literate, intelligent, insightful, and entertaining novel draws to a close." Cheryl Merser of *USA Today* was similarly impressed with Smith's "beautiful letters," though she found the novel's epistolary format unsatisfying in places. While *Fair and Tender Ladies* was not named to bestseller lists at the time of its release, it has been published in several editions and remains in print two decades after its initial publication. The novel has also taken on a life beyond the page, inspiring Barbara Bates Smith's one-woman play *I Remane, Forever, Ivy Rowe*. Though Bates Smith's production drew mixed reviews—the *New York Times*'s Mel Gussow called a 1991 performance only "intermittently . . . evocative"—it has enjoyed lasting popularity: Bates Smith estimates that she has performed as Ivy more than seven hundred times for more than twenty years.

Literacy and Identity

From her earliest letters, Ivy makes apparent her commitment to and love for the written word. The first lines of *Fair and Tender Ladies,* in fact, read: "Your name is not much common here, I think it is so pretty too. I say it now and agin it tastes sweet in my mouth like honey or cane" (11). Words are beautiful to Ivy even when her life is not, and they stimulate her senses in uncommon ways. However, Ivy's devotion to reading and writing goes beyond aesthetic enjoyment. Ivy depends upon her literacy to establish and nurture her very identity, working through dilemmas and decisions in the letters she writes. Ivy retells stories of her family and region and creates her own stories as she goes, making a place for herself in the storytelling tradition of her mountain homeland. When difficult times in life threaten to overwhelm Ivy, it is these stories that sustain her, restoring her to life as she both hears and writes them.

Because of the isolated surroundings in which she is raised, her family and friends identify Ivy as a prodigious writer of letters. She initially relies on her teacher and family members to transport letters to their recipients, a necessity that, in addition to making the community aware of the frequency with which Ivy sends letters, also compromises the privacy of her communications. Her first letter to Hanneke, a would-be pen pal, for instance, is returned to her by her teacher Mrs. Brown because she deems its subject matter inappropriate. Ivy's position as a young girl in a rural community makes her commitment to writing her honest thoughts more difficult to sustain. Further impeding her writing is her family's poverty, which requires that Ivy perform a number of tiring chores at Sugar Fork. "Momma gets pitched off iffen I read too much," Ivy writes in her very first letter. "I have to holp out and I will just fill my head with notions, Momma says it will do me no good in the end" (15).

Although Ivy's writing establishes her identity in her family and community, it is not always viewed positively. As a child, Ivy's habit of writing is seen as a damaging and even a dangerous thing, a path to unattainable dreams and unavoidable disappointment. "In the same way that Aldous Rife warns Richard not to become involved with Dory since at best he can only create longings that her life can never fulfill," Erica Abrams Locklear argues, "Ivy's mother becomes upset with Ivy's constant reading" (196). However, as she ages and the mountains she calls home evolve, Ivy's writing becomes a novelty that, while still uncommon, carries less of a stigma. "I am old and crazy," Ivy writes in one of her last letters; "I have got things to think on and letters to write" (303). Without children to care for or a mother to assist, Ivy's writing stops being seen as a distraction from productivity.

Ivy's writing is characteristic of her identity, and it is also a tool by which she explores other components of her selfhood. The critic Tanya Long Bennett, for instance, argues that Ivy's letter writing affords her the opportunity to try on different identities and ideologies, deconstructing and shedding them as she writes about them. Ivy "fluctuates between acceptance and rejection of the ideologies that influence her," Bennett writes, thereby creating and revealing her "fluid self" ("Protean Ivy" 76). By her use of that term Bennett suggests that Ivy subscribes to a system of relativism and causality rather than to one of universal truths. Ivy offers some support for this characterization in her later letters, telling her daughter Joli that "the older I get, the more different things seem natural enough to me. I take a real big view!" (279). Still, though Ivy is open-minded and conscious of the complexities inherent in things and people, she also expresses her belief in the "essential" nature of people. In the very same letter she writes that "the true nature will come out whether or no, we have all got a true nature and we can't hide it, it will pop out when you least expect it" (279). Ivy is a woman open to surprise, possibility, and variety in life, but she is not such a relativist to deny the existence of truths.

George Hovis offers a similar interpretation of Ivy's writing as it relates to her selfhood, arguing that that Ivy has an "emerging postmodern consciousness: she takes a progressively eclectic approach in understanding her life, basing her interpretations in one moment on the model of a folk narrative and in the next on nineteenth-century British gothic novels" (162). Like Bennett, he notes the ways Ivy resists easy categorization by drawing from diverse ideologies and sources in the formation of her self. Hovis adds, however, that Ivy "conceives of herself in terms of a present self and a past self, and she consistently privileges her girlhood, . . . imagining a continuity of experience between her girlhood and her present self" (172). This profession is borne out, Hovis argues, by Ivy's marriage to Oakley and her return to her parents' home on Sugar Fork, where she initially lives a life not unlike her mother's.

An especially striking technique that Ivy uses to establish her identity in both her letters and her life is her creation of "doubles" for herself, figures who, Bennett has written, "mirror a part of [Ivy] she could not otherwise see" (94). Silvaney and Honey Breeding, particularly, are figures that live life without some of the restrictions that Ivy has; they are, in Ivy's letters, near-mythic characters through whom she lives vicariously. Katherine Kearns lays out the particulars of Ivy's strategy: "Silvaney is a conduit to carry away madness, the sacrificial figure who remains necessary for the female artist to survive. Thus exercised, Ivy may accommodate the world without going mad" (190). Ivy is too rooted at Sugar Fork to travel as does Honey Breeding and too practical to wander the woods like Silvaney, yet her connection to both characters nourishes the parts of her identity that long for their respective freedoms of movement.

Though critics might quibble in their interpretations of the ways in which Ivy defines herself through her writing, there is no disagreement that she does capture her identity in letters. When she weighs whether or not to travel to Boston with her teacher Miss Torrington, for instance, Ivy writes a letter that provides insight into her dilemma. Ivy sees her Granny Rowe and Aunt Tennessee as she speaks with an elegant neighbor and later writes Silvaney: "I confess that for a minute I drew back, for here was Granny smoking her pipe and wearing her old mans hat, and Tennessee behind her giggling and clutching that filthy dirty crazy bead purse. I drew back. For all of a sudden they seemed to me strange people out of another time, I could not breth. . . . And I was ashamed of myself. And I thought, If I go to Boston, I will not see them, nor Beaulahs new baby, nor Ethel grinning behind that big cash register" (107).

Ivy recognizes here that her choice to go to Boston is not based solely on geography or education. Studying in Boston with the refined Miss Torrington will separate her, forever, from the uneducated, unsophisticated family and culture she has loved. As Locklear puts it, Ivy grapples, in passages such as this, with "her entry into a different social class and discourse community and also an awareness of the impending conflicted family relationships resulting from that transition" (197). The tug-of-war between the community of her birth and the wider world runs through Ivy's letters as she seeks to find her place in these very different realms. Ultimately, Ivy remains near her mountain homeland for her whole life, causing, as Locklear notes, "her literacy campaign [to operate] within her primary discourse community. . . . While this allows Ivy to avoid the perils of attaining multiple literacies, it also limits her empowerment" (203). Ivy does not gain material advantage by her reading and writing; instead she reaps the more abstract but important benefits of greater self-knowledge and connection to her family's cultural and historical roots.

In her study of Appalachian women's literacies, Locklear provides useful analyses of Ivy's literacy and the problems and joys it creates in her life. She notes, primarily, that Ivy's writing "represents a blending of the oral and the literate that marks a progression in voice for [Smith's] readers" (195). Unlike *Black Mountain Breakdown*'s Crystal Spangler, whose story is written for her, or *Oral History*'s Granny Younger, who speaks her story but does not write it, Ivy visually represents her own speech. Doing so allows her to privilege the oral even as she records it; by writing her letters in a voice that presumably resembles her spoken one, Ivy creates a written record imbued with the feeling and truth that Smith usually reserves for characters' oral narratives. For the first time Smith's female protagonist is doing both the talking and the writing, providing, as Dorothy Dodge Robbins has observed, "an examination of an oral culture, not usurped by, but in transition to its written counterpart" (136). Smith underscores the importance of Ivy's recording her own words early in the novel, when Ivy visits the house of her teacher Mrs. Brown. Ivy avoids telling one of her favorite stories to Mrs. Brown's husband because, she says, "sometimes when I say things, Mister Brown writes them down in his notebook and then I feel like whatever I have said isn't mine any more, it's a funny feeling" (54). Ivy recognizes here that her family's stories lose an element of authenticity when recorded by a "foreigner," that these stories are meant to be shared orally, in the voice of someone from Ivy's mountains.

Although letters provide the structure for the entirety of *Fair and Tender Ladies,* Ivy frequently reminds readers—and herself—that they are important only while they are being created. When she is near death, for instance, Ivy burns piles of letters she has saved. Explaining her actions to Joli, she writes that "the letters didn't mean anything. Not to the dead girl Silvaney, of course—nor to me. Nor had they ever. It was the writing of them, that signified" (313). Bennett points out that by burning bundles of her letters, Ivy frees herself from written definition. This act, too, is consistent with Ivy's awareness of the importance of the writing process itself and with Smith's promotion of private art as equal to its public counterparts. Burning insures that most of Ivy's letters will never be published or even read by others. "With every one I burned," Ivy writes, "my soul grew lighter, lighter, as if it rose too with the smoke." Ivy's identity is tied to writing and self-expression but not to the letters themselves.

Ivy's letters are a place in which she creates and retells stories, and it is this specific function of self-expression that makes her writing necessary for her survival. Sharing stories saves Ivy's life in a literal sense. For instance, when Ivy, busy with five children and her home on Sugar Fork, stops writing her letters and feels the lack of a storyteller in her life, the effect of these absences on her is undeniably physical. "Nothing but skin and bones," Ivy imagines herself "a dried up husk . . . leeched out by hard work and babies" (187). The stories that Ivy hears fuel her own storytelling in letters, and her decisions about what kinds of stories to repeat are decisions that profoundly shape her life. While she adores and internalizes the folktales of the Cline sisters, she gently critiques her daughter Joli's writing for its lack of a strong love story. "It was pretty good," she writes, "although I think you could of used more of a love interest" (290). Ivy's capacity for love and joy drives her interest in romance, which informs the original stories that she writes. By creating narratives about Silvaney, Honey Breeding, and others, she is better able to understand and to live within the often difficult spaces of her life. Beginning with the story of her parents' elopement and their establishment of a home at Sugar Fork, Ivy infuses her letters with stories old and new.

Ivy learns to rely on storytelling for strength during her difficult childhood, during which she lives with her sickly, dying father and overworked, broken mother. After recording the story of her parents' marriage and arrival at Sugar Fork, Ivy writes, "Now I am glad I have set this all down for I can see my Momma and Daddy as young, and laghing [*sic*]. This is not how they are today" (14). Ivy benefits from reminders of the hopeful beginning her parents enjoyed; this strategy of recording or reciting familiar stories is one that Ivy frequently uses in her letters. As Hovis observes, it is Ivy's ability to "recreate the past, internalizing and reconfiguring it by means of alternative narratives of

her life, rather than being overwhelmed by a static mythology located outside
and beyond herself" that "indicates the nature of Ivy's triumph" (167).

Hovis thoroughly examines Ivy's frequent referencing of her parents' story,
calling it an attempt to make her own "creation myth." By adding her own
details to her parents' story, he argues, Ivy "selectively refine[s] the details of
the story and even invent[s] missing details to satisfy . . . psychological needs."
For instance, when Ivy describes her heavy workload to Hanneke in a letter,
she "turns what might seem a detriment into the defining attribute of Sugar
Fork" (168). Ivy describes her work in positive terms, explaining how "we grow
nearabout all we eat. . . . We raise what we need, we don't go to the store for
nothing but coffee and shoes and nails and to get the mail" (16). Hovis calls
this description a testament to Ivy's reverence for values of "self-sufficiency
and independence." These values connect Ivy with her mother, Maude, who
often tells Ivy that she, Maude, will not be beholden to anyone. They also fuel
her appreciation of the storytelling Cline sisters, "maiden ladys" who live in a
"dolly cabin with everything just so." When they visit Ivy's family to tell stories
on Christmas night, Ivy writes, "Don't nobody know how they live exackly
Daddy said, they do not farm nor raise a thing but beans and flowers . . . I think
myself they live on storys, they do not need much food" (33). Ivy believes that
the sisters magically are self-sufficient, exempt from the pain and suffering that
comes with her own family's strategies for survival.

Ivy's magical thinking has a similar impact on readers of Smith's novel.
Though the events of Ivy's life are often challenging and can be painful to
read, her narration is so spirited that it sometimes obscures the tragedy that is
on the page. When Ivy describes the death of Lonnie Rash, for instance, she
addresses her pain, writing that "Lonnie is dead in the war, it has upset me so!
(146). However, she quickly turns her attention to describing baby Joli after
mentioning Lonnie, writing "You ought to see Joli, she is so beautiful!" It is significant that Ivy makes these statements in a letter to Silvaney, from whom she
hides nothing. Clearly, Ivy is not simply directing her letter to a happier subject
out of consideration for her reader's happiness. In conversation with Silvaney
Ivy writes as she thinks and is thus illustrating one of her coping strategies.
Until she becomes depressed at age forty, Ivy possesses an infectious ability to
smooth over the most difficult events of her life.

Female Identity and Home

Before its publication, *Fair and Tender Ladies* was titled "Letters from Home."
Though the original title was less poetic than the eventual one, it referenced
one of the novel's most distinguishing features, Ivy's permanent residence in
the mountains of Southeastern Virginia. Ivy moves short distances within the

mountains—to the town of Majestic, to a mining town called Diamond, and, briefly, to a Bristol hospital—but she never lives far from her birthplace. Thus all of her letters are drafted from the same small corner of Appalachia, though they make their way to destinations from Florida to Holland. Several factors contribute to Ivy's decision to remain in the mountains, many of which stem directly from the fact that Ivy is a woman rather than a man. Despite an intense desire to travel, Ivy is yoked by children, circumstance, and love to the family home on Sugar Fork. Though it is easy to see that Ivy's relative physical stasis is a limitation in her life, Smith often suggests that it actually strengthens Ivy's writing and her identity. As Paula Gallant Eckard observes, Ivy's connection to the mountains is reflected in the structure of the novel, which is split into sections based on the places Ivy lives. "By creating an alignment between Ivy's female experiences and these various mountain locales," she writes, "Smith demonstrates how a woman's life is often inextricably bound to place and reveals the profound identification that Appalachian women share with their mountain surroundings" (*Maternal* 159).

Even as she remains near Sugar Fork, Ivy repeatedly underscores her keen interest in cultures and persons far from her Appalachian home. From her longing to communicate with her Dutch pen pal Hanneke to her fascination with the ever-traveling Honey Breeding, Ivy seeks new sources for information about the world. This curiosity has led the critic Tena Helton to call Ivy a "conduit between mountain and outside cultures" who "overcomes an apparent lack to mobility, creating an integrated, 'rooted' identity by traveling through the stories of her home and by contact with outsiders and their cultural differences" (5). Helton's observation supports Bennett's and Hovis's characterizations of Ivy's identity as "fluid" and "postmodern," respectively, as it implies that she merges diverse influences in the making of herself. Though Ivy is a permanent resident of Appalachia, her writing and her curiosity give her an understanding of the wider world.

Ivy's fascination with places she thinks are more exciting than her mountain home leads her to consider living in one of those places. She imagines two scenarios: in one she pursues her education with Gertrude Torrington in Boston; in the other she takes off downriver with young men in the lumber industry. Though one of these trips is more practical than the other, Ivy's hopes of both ventures are dashed because she is a girl. Her choice to sleep with Lonnie Rash leads to a pregnancy before she can depart for Boston, and she would never be allowed to join the young men on the river. As Debbie Wesley has written, however, Ivy's inability to go to Boston is not necessarily a bad thing. "Ivy does not lose her art by losing Miss Torrington," she argues, "who represents the kind of pretentious, institutionalized, isolated art that Smith wishes to avoid. Ivy continues to write her letters, and her pregnancy appears to feed her art rather than stifle it" (93). By staying close to the stories with which she has grown up, Ivy avoids having her unique voice molded into something more conventional.

In a letter to Silvaney, Ivy addresses the other trip she longs to undertake, describing the journey that young men make downriver soon after her arrival in town. Tasked with moving lumber from Virginia to Kentucky, the men ride rafts of logs along the river before undertaking a four-day walk back to Majestic. "I wuld give anything to be one of them boys and ride the rafts down to Kentucky on the great spring tide," Ivy writes. "I have even thought of waring jeans and a boys shirt and shoes and trying to sneak along, but Momma and Geneva wuld have a fit" (91). Though Ivy sees opportunities for travel at this point in the novel, she is nevertheless conscious that this sort of rough trip is not something she can ever undertake. Ivy's inability to make this trip has less of an upside than her inability to travel to Boston. Rather than insulating her writing from the influence of formality, the forces that keep Ivy from the river merely limit her experience within the mountains, relegating her to activities and pursuits deemed suitable for a woman.

The degree to which Ivy's sex limits her mobility fluctuates as she ages. In Ivy's girlhood, for instance, her opportunities to travel tend to be tied to her desire to gain experience or education. She ventures to her teacher Mrs. Brown's house, then dreams of studying with Miss Torrington in Boston or exploring the river. Later in Ivy's life, though, her chances to leave mountain life depend more on her relationships with men: she refuses a wild life with Franklin Ransom, she is denied a nomadic life with Honey Breeding, and she rejects her late sister's husband, Curtis Bostick, when he begs her to go off and marry him. The exception to this pattern is when Ivy is invited to the wedding of her daughter Joli in eastern Virginia, but even then it is Oakley who dissuades her from attending. "Oakley does not feel up to the trip, plain and simple," she writes Silvaney; he "feels we ought not to go, and in my heart of hearts I know he is right" (268). Ivy will not travel with men like Franklin and Curtis, and she cannot travel with the men she would like to accompany, Honey or Oakley. In her old age, when Ivy is encouraged by many to leave Sugar Fork and has the flexibility to do so, she instead feels compelled to remain there. "I am old and crazy," she writes to Silvaney; "I have a need to be up here on this mountain again and sit looking out as I look out now at the mountains" (301).

The societal and familial expectations that keep Ivy close to Sugar Fork as a young woman are eventually more forcefully imposed by Ivy's responsibilities as a wife to Oakley and a mother to her many children. Ivy does not avoid travel and adventure only because they seem inappropriate: her access to such experience is limited by the necessity that she care for her family's home and nurse her children, much as her own mother Maude did years earlier. "I must of knowed it from childhood," Ivy writes to Silvaney, describing how hard the work of raising a family and farming at Sugar Fork is, "from watching it kill Daddy first, then Momma. But that is the thing about being young—you never think that what happened to anybody else might happen to you, too" (201). Ivy explicitly acknowledges that the life she has chosen prevents her from traveling much. She writes: "I never get out and go places any more, Silvaney. A woman just can't go off and leave so many children; . . . it seems like I don't want to do a thing when I'm not working, except rest" (195).

Thus Ivy's womanhood does not just prevent her from leaving home; it also impedes her exploration of the place where she lives. Ivy emphasizes this again decades after she is unable to pilot logs down the river. When Ivy and Honey Breeding climb to the very top of Blue Star Mountain, where she has lived for most of forty years, Ivy writes: "All of a sudden I thought, I could of climbed up here by myself, anytime! But I had not. I remembered as girls how you and me would beg to go hunting on the mountain, Silvaney, but they said, That is for boys. Or how we wanted to go up there after berries and they'd say, Wait till Victor can take you, or Wait till Daddy gets home. . . . And I had got up there myself at long last with a man it is true, but not a man like any I had ever seen before in all my life" (233).

As spirited and independent as she often is, Ivy has never taken the initiative to climb Blue Star herself but feels empowered when she finally ascends the peak with Honey. "I felt giddy and crazy climbing the mountain," she writes Silvaney. "It seemed I was dropping years as I went, letting them fall there beside the trace, leaving them all behind me" (224). This passage is similar to the one in which Ivy burns her letters: both experiences leave her feeling lighter. Though she ultimately cannot leave her mountain home behind, climbing higher than her earlier personal history and doing something she was told she could not because of her gender are cathartic and healing for her.

Despite her desire to be relieved of the heavier aspects of her past, Ivy continues to cultivate her ties to family and home. As Hovis observes, her residence at her childhood home is self-perpetuating. "Ivy remains geographically rooted at Sugar Fork," he writes, "reinvesting the landscape with memories of her family and making it ever harder to leave" (167). By eking out a life at Sugar Fork even after Oakley's passing, Ivy continues what has become something of a family tradition for the women to whom she is related. Granny Rowe, Aunt Tenessee, Virgie and Gaynelle Cline, and Ivy's mother Maude all attempt to maintain their lives in Ivy's mountains without the help of men, with varying degrees of success. In this way Ivy's family history is a matrilineal one, centered on home and stories and love, which Ivy feels bound to continue. "The water is still as cold and as pure as it ever was," Ivy writes upon her return to Sugar Fork with Oakley; "it tastes as good as it did to Momma when she and Daddy stopped to drink, riding Lightning" (187). Helton has called Ivy's decision to make her home on Sugar Fork a "search for connection with her mother," whose external life her own so resembles" (10). Helton persuasively argues that although Ivy sets out to follow her father's example—farming, telling stories, appreciating the land—her lot is more like her mother's, characterized by the hard work of bearing and sustaining many children on a rural homestead.

Ivy's association of Sugar Fork with the women who have preceded her in the mountains is also influenced by her relationship with her sister Silvaney, who was institutionalized before Ivy's move to Majestic. Silvaney is no longer at Sugar Fork when Ivy returns, but, as Hill has written, she is strongly associated with it by her name and her untamed behavior. When Ivy is at Sugar Fork, she has to face the creek where she found her brother Babe dead and the chest where her late mother's "berrying quilt" lies. But she is also close to her memories of Silvaney, who functions as a sort of "double" for Ivy even after Silvaney has died. While memories themselves are significant, Ivy's need for Silvaney is more than sentimental. As Kearns argues, "Silvaney is a conduit to carry away madness, the sacrificial figure who remains necessary for the female artist to survive. Thus exorcised, Ivy may accommodate the world without going mad" (190).

If Silvaney saves Ivy from madness, Ivy's experiences with motherhood and loss nearly drive her to it. During her first pregnancy Ivy feels "helplessly bound to her body and place," and imagines that she is trapped, trying to escape, in her own womb (Locklear 202). She stops feeling entrapped after Joli is born, but the feeling returns once Ivy has married Oakley and returned to Sugar Fork. She is pregnant for most of her twenties, bearing babies live and stillborn. Both bind her deeply to Sugar Fork. She must care for the living—six of her own children, plus a friend's daughter and eventually a grandson—and tread the ground where the dead lie. "Now I have got two little babies on Pilgrim Knob," Ivy writes Silvaney; "I never gave them a name. But I remember losing them and getting them both, I remember everything" (203). Though Ivy loves her children, her responsibilities and sad memories leave her in a damaged place; "marriage and repeated childbearing," Eckard notes, "impose silence and a loss of language" (169). Ivy does not write for years at a time, and the effect of her loss of language and expression is palpable. Her youngest nursing baby seems to be "sucking [her] life right out of [her]," and she feels lost in a "great soft darkness" (194). Dark as it is, Ivy's depression gives her a better understanding of her own mother Maude and briefly reconnects her with her father's mother, Granny Rowe, who tries to build up Ivy's strength. When neither connection is enough to save her, Ivy turns again to Silvaney, to whom she writes "with a vengeance." As Eckard observes, Ivy "uses her letters to Silvaney as a way to write out of the body, out of the darkness and fatigue in which she has been immersed" (170).

What ultimately pulls Ivy out of her depression is her restorative affair with Honey Breeding. "It is like I've had an electric shock," she writes to Silvaney. "For the first time, I know, I am on fire" (210). When Ivy climbs Blue Star Mountain with him, she has language and sexuality both restored to her. Nancy C. Parrish explains this restoration when she writes that "Honey's storytelling enriches Ivy's existence by helping her hear—not the silence of a black oblivion—but the stories that are in her 'very own head'" ("Rescue" 119). Ivy's attention to the sound of her own voice underscores this point. Though she delights in listening to Honey Breeding's stories, she is most amazed by her own voice, which "sounded funny in [her] ears. It sounded rusty" (224). Ivy returns from her escape with Honey Breeding with renewed command of that voice and a new ability to balance her responsibilities as a mother with invigorating sexuality. However, Kearns argues that "while, for Ivy, finally, maternity and art are mutually generative, Smith's compromise remains as always before in the direction of maternal selfishness" (192). Ivy's daughter LuIda suddenly dies while Ivy is away with Honey Breeding, an event that Ivy—and her community—cannot help but connect with her absence. Ivy grieves LuIda's death, but, as Hovis points out, she "does not sink to the depths of self-absorption and abstraction that she had reached before her affair with Honey Breeding" (175).

Ivy is the first protagonist in a Lee Smith novel to provide an in-depth description of her experiences with pregnancy and young motherhood as they happen; she also is among the first mothers in Smith's fiction to narrate her own story. After presenting appearance-obsessed mothers in her first four novels, and mostly voiceless mothers in *Oral History* and *Family Linen,* Smith finally, as Eckard argues, finds "a discourse that is close to the maternal body, one that replicates the natural cadences of life, language, and female bodily experience" (173). Smith draws on Ivy to fictionalize motherhood again in *The Christmas Letters* and, especially, *On Agate Hill.* Still, the immediacy and impact of Ivy's maternal story are unique in Smith's fiction.

Spirituality, Sexuality, and That Old-Time Religion

Ivy's identification with her mountain homeland also extends to her spiritual life. The tension between traditional religious experience and the elemental, naturalistic spirituality of Lee Smith's treatment of her mountains frequently arises in *Fair and Tender Ladies.* Never a true believer in the traditional Christian faith as presented to her by instructors, evangelists, and her husband, Ivy instead finds comfort and fulfillment in the land that surrounds her. Water, in all its forms, proves especially evocative for Ivy, a woman who lives without ever seeing the ocean; at difficult or poignant moments in her life, Ivy often feels comforted by the glint of light from an icicle or from water beaded on leaves. As she reflects on spirituality in her letters, Ivy records the moments when it intersects with sexuality in ways discomfiting and sublime. In an interview with Susan Ketchin, Lee Smith explained how Ivy's difficulty accepting the tenets of Christianity was influenced by Smith's own experience. "Ivy is like me," she said, "unable to find a religion that suits her—an organized religion. She makes up her own. Writing for her is sort of like it has been for me—a sort of a saving thing. Almost a religion of its own" (135).

Though Ivy frequently changes her mind about some subjects, she consistently expresses her disillusionment with Christianity. At age twelve she assertively states her feelings about the Christian God in a letter to Mrs. Brown. "I do not pray, nor do I think much of God," Ivy writes; "It is not rigt what he sends on people. He sends too much to bare" (39). Reeling from the death of her father, Ivy does not deny the existence of God; instead she proclaims her disappointment with his behavior. Later, she has cause for disappointment in the men who claim to represent God's interest. The Christian evangelists with whom Ivy speaks are uniformly scoundrels, traveling men whose fervent sermons are matched in intensity only by their hypocrisy. Sam Russell Sage, the first evangelist she encounters, accepts money from Ivy's wealthy grandfather in exchange for burying her mother on his land instead of near Sugar Fork, as she had wished. Ivy's self-important brother Garnie is no better, cruelly blaming Ivy for the death of her daughter LuIda before attempting to whip her with his belt. "If Sam Russell Sage is who God has sent," Ivy writes Silvaney, "then I don't know if I even want to be saved ether, in spite of the firey hand!" (102). Ivy connects Christianity to the domineering and patriarchal behavior of the men who preach it in her community.

Still, Ivy does not generally condemn or disdain practitioners of Christianity. She respects the faith of her husband Oakley and enjoys reading from the little white Bible left behind by Garnie. "I go to church with Oakley sometimes," she writes, and "it is the only time I ever see a break in the lines of his face" (247). In her final letter she intersperses lines from Ecclesiastes with memories and visions from her life. Ivy enjoys the poetry in portions of the Bible even as she denies the centrality of its tenets in her life. Language, as it so often does for her, bridges two elements that she otherwise struggles to reconcile. "Ecclesiastes is good and makes sense," Ivy writes; "I like to read Ecclesiastes and run my hand along the fine-grained wood of this deer that Oakley cut out of a poplar stump, it makes me think I am close to him" (302). In passages such as this Ivy mixes words from the Bible with emotions grounded in her life and with material taken from the land that is so important in her own version of spirituality.

Ivy also sees implicit connections between religious fervor and sexual excitement. She first makes the connection as a teenager in Majestic, where she lives in a boardinghouse and observes Sage, the pious evangelist, bedding her mother's friend. Ivy feels "the firey hand of God clutching [her] in the stomach" during one of Sage's sermons and initially interprets this feeling as a sign from God that she should be saved (100). She changes her mind, though, after learning about Sage's womanizing and beginning an affair of her own with Lonnie Rash: Ivy "let him put his tonge way down in [her] mouth and the firey hand grabbed [her] for good" (103). Having experienced the same feeling when sexually and spiritually aroused, Ivy decides that the "firey hand" actually is a warning from God that she is "bad" (95). Here Ivy echoes the moral confusion of Charlotte Brontë's *Jane Eyre*. As H. H. Campbell notes, Jane, too, feels "'a hand of fiery iron'" when "undergoing her ordeal of deciding whether or not to leave Rochester" (141). Ivy's confusion is only compounded when her Presbyterian missionary teacher Miss Torrington kisses her. Ivy has sex with Lonnie Rash for the first time immediately after the kiss but ultimately rejects his claim to her, as well as Miss Torrington's.

Ivy saves the devotion that she refuses Christianity for the mountain landscape she inhabits. In the same letter in which she expresses disappointment in God about her father's death, Ivy describes the walk to her father's gravesite: "It was the softest palest prettiest morning. Everything smelt so new because of the rain, it was like Genesis in the Bible. . . . Somehow in the pale perly ligt these apple trees seemed the prettiest I have ever seed them, and smelled the sweetest, and this on the day we berried my daddy wich shuld of been the worstest in my life, but somehow it was not" (48).

In the natural world Ivy finds the comfort that she does not find through prayer or salvation by God, and she explicitly recognizes that her surroundings are part of something divine. By comparing the trip to bury her father to "Genesis in the Bible," Ivy shows how her mountains make her "feel like church," a turn of phrase she uses later in life to describe breakfast with her family. Ivy adapts the language of Christianity to explain the feelings the natural world inspires in her.

Ivy associates many of these poignant moments with water in all its states of matter. As Bennett has written, water "can work to create a sort of transcendental moment for Ivy" ("The Protean Ivy" 80). Like the rain on the day of her father's burial, ice impacts her mood and outlook on the world. "The whole world was news," she thinks, looking out on an icy morning, "and it was like I was the onliest person that had ever looked upon it, and it was mine" (18).

Like Ivy, who writes that she has "been so many people" in her life, water is changeable yet constant, able to convert to different states while retaining its basic identity as water. Ivy appreciates water when she sees it, and yearns for it when she cannot access it, as when the young men pilot logs downriver from Majestic. "The river is brown and swirly," Ivy writes to Silvaney; "it has waves and foams up the bank" (91). Though this description is not as alluring as Ivy's writing about rainy mornings or glittering ice, Ivy is drawn to its subject anyway. The possibilities water offers capture her imagination, even when they are murky.

Though Ivy never makes a trip down the river, she does gain greater knowledge of her spiritual self through traveling her mountains. Her climb to the top of Blue Star with Honey Breeding, for instance, helps her to recognize her own agency, power, and spirit, things she had forgotten among the chaos and exhaustion of childrearing. Interestingly, her time with Honey Breeding may also be the only time that Ivy places something above the landscape in terms of its sacred value to her. As Hovis argues, Honey's presence "becomes so real to [Ivy] that he obscures the landscape," an event that Ivy believes leads to the death of her daughter LuIda. "Ivy has replaced her mother's narrative of Edenic harmony with the figure of Honey Breeding," Hovis argues, "and a new story in which Ivy leaves her family to pursue her own private fantasy (175).

Ivy's story about Honey Breeding is just one of many that she adds to her collection of sacred, mostly oral texts about her homeland. The story of Whitebear Whittington, for instance, is recalled by Ivy throughout the novel and even colors her feelings toward some of the people whom she meets. Though Whitebear, a handsome man by night and a bear by day, calls Honey Breeding to mind—he wanders the mountains, roaming the hills for seven years while his beloved searches for him—Ivy also associates the story of Whitebear with her "wild" uncle, Revel Rowe. "When I grow up and become a writter," Ivy says, "I will write of a man like my uncle Revel who can come like a storm in the nigt and knock a born lady off her feet" (80). A mule trader by day, Revel is a ladies' man and "antic" by night, a drinker of whiskey, a storyteller, and a musician. Though Ivy romanticizes Revel's exploits, she identifies with his plight as an artist who spends much of his time doing work he does not love. Ivy evokes Revel in her final letter as she describes Whitebear Whittington: "He lives there even now I tell you and he is wild, wild. He runs thogh the night with his eyes on fire and no one can take him" (315). Though Ivy builds her life with the stable Christian man Oakley, she feels a deep connection with dangerous, passionate men like Honey, Revel, and the fictional Whitebear.

Ivy's mountain spiritualism also has associated rituals to accompany its mythology and stories. When Ivy is experiencing postpartum depression, the ancient-seeming Granny Rowe takes her hunting in the mountains for iron-rich greens to eat. "You have got to purify your blood," Granny tells Ivy (195). Although there is a scientific reason that greens are beneficial for a woman like Ivy, Granny does not know about it; she knows the ritual and its effect and passes it along to Ivy so that she, too, can perform it. Katerina Prajznerová has pointed out that many of the medicinal plants whose utility Granny Rowe extolls are also important in Cherokee culture, which references a mythology in which "preserving natural balance in the world" is "central" (29).

As Ivy upholds some of her community's nature-based practices, she also adds to them by taking steps to preserve Sugar Fork. Beginning when she witnesses the abuse that mining companies inflict on her land and their employees, Ivy stands against commercial invasion of her sacred space. She puts a "No Trespassing" sign on her land to prevent the Peabody Coal Company from mining it; when the "bulldozer man" ignores her sign, she threatens him at gunpoint until he departs (306). Ivy's devotion to the land is poetic but not just abstract. At novel's end Ivy and Dreama Fox, Oakley's sister, live alone in the house on Sugar Fork. Ivy's children live in others places, and her siblings are dead or dispersed. There is a sense that when Ivy leaves Sugar Fork—and her departure is almost certainly imminent as she writes her last letter—the mountain home will simply cease to exist, at least in the day-to-day lives of Ivy's family.

Though Ivy's home and letters will have ceased to exist by the time of her death, there is hope within Smith's intratextual narrative that some of what Ivy stood for and sought to preserve will live on. By novel's end Ivy's daughter Joli has become the author that Ivy long wished to be, and, much to her mother's chagrin, she writes of Appalachia. Joli should, according to Ivy, write about New York instead of "these mountains which nobody wants to read about" (290). Ivy does not recognize the artistry of her life, private as it has been and is likely to remain. But, as Smith suggests in other fiction—"Cakewalk" and "The Happy Memories Club," particularly—Ivy's unread letters and authentically lived life constitute art in their own right. With Ivy, Smith created a protagonist for whom mirrors are a thing of beauty rather than fear. As Kearns puts it, Ivy illustrates "the metamorphosis in Smith's fiction from anxiety and ambivalence to empowerment and from there to self-documentation, with its implicit valuation of its subject" (193).

CHAPTER 5

Old Crazy Stories One More Time
Lee Smith in the 1990s

Coming off the career-defining success of *Oral History* and *Fair and Tender Ladies,* Smith began the 1990s as an established writer—assured, acclaimed, and no longer squeezing writing in between other jobs. Though she taught creative writing at North Carolina State University, at various workshops, and at the Hindman Settlement School during this decade, her work was beneficial to, rather than competitive with, her writing career. She published prolifically in the 1990s. *Me and My Baby View the Eclipse* (1990), *The Devil's Dream* (1992), *Saving Grace* (1995), *The Christmas Letters* (1996), and *News of the Spirit* (1997), though less critically lauded than her most admired books, are challenging and inventive. Smith addresses a diverse variety of subjects in them —rural Pentecostalism, the history of country music, and motherhood are just a few—but the works all feature strong character voices and, usually, the perspectives of multiple narrators.

Smith's novels of the 1990s are more ambitious in scope than many of her earlier works and also more specific and localized in terms of their settings. Whereas Smith allowed that the plot of her first novel *The Last Day the Dogbushes Bloomed*, for instance, could be set in "any small town," the external spaces inhabited by Smith's characters are more distinctive and consequential in her later works. Usually these settings are the mountains of Virginia or North Carolina, although characters occasionally venture to the coast or other southern states. "It wasn't until *Black Mountain Breakdown*," Smith has said, "that I decided to really write about the mountains" (Tate 3). Since the publication of that novel in 1980, every novel Smith has published has been at set in the mountains, whether wholly, as in 1988's *Fair and Tender Ladies,* or partially, as in 2006's Civil War–era *On Agate Hill.* Smith's refined focus gave her space to use the wealth of Appalachian stories, songs, and anecdotes she remembered, recorded, and researched.

Changes in her community and personal life prompted Smith's literary return to the mountains. Her divorce and remarriage, the losses of her parents and her adult son Josh, and the intentional flooding and rebuilding of Grundy each impacted her textual choices, in ways conscious and subconscious, in small details and thematic concerns. The apparent choices are particularly prevalent in *The Christmas Letters,* in which many references come undisguised from Smith's own life. One character in the novella, Mary Copeland, writes and distributes a newsletter as a child; the publication is called the *Small Review,* just as Smith's own childhood newsletter was, and includes an article identically titled to one of Smith's own. As an adult Mary reflects on having "written out [her] life story in recipes," dividing time into "the Cool Whip and mushroom soup years, the hibachi and fondue period, then the quiche and crepes phase, and now it's these salsa years" (101). Smith repeats this line almost verbatim while describing her own experience, and likens the experience to that of her mother, in the *Dimestore* essay "Recipe Box" (39). The subconscious influences on her fiction are also helpfully explicated in *Dimestore,* where Smith explains how such elements work their way into her stories. "No matter what I may think I am writing about at any given time," Smith says, "I have come to realize that it is all, finally, about me, often in some complicated way I won't come to understand until years later" (169).

For the large project of memorializing Grundy, much of which was demolished in 2005, Smith turned to nonfiction, editing the oral history *Sitting on the Courthouse Bench* (2000). The book was hastened by the Grundy Flood Control and Redevelopment Project, but it had its beginnings in Smith's long-term interest in recording something of her hometown. In *Dimestore* Smith notes how she began in the 1980s "to tape my relatives and elderly mountain friends, collecting the old stories, songs, and histories in earnest, with the aim of preserving the type of speech—Appalachian English—and the ways of life of a bygone era" (175). Smith's own introduction to the book, in which she relates childhood memories of Grundy, underscores her dedication to preserving the town's character by recording its vernacular. "In this book we are simply telling our own stories in our own words," she writes, "in the belief that our voices will blend to create a vibrant testimony to the life of this whole community" (18). As she does in her fiction, Smith privileges oral testimony in *Sitting on the Courthouse Bench.*

Across nuanced settings Smith's later fictions share thematic concerns. Chief among these concerns is religion, which often factors in Smith's novels and stories but reaches the forefront of many of her works in the 1990s. In interviews and in her autobiographical writing, Smith makes it clear that Christianity and, more generally, spirituality have been as integral to her personal life as they are to her fiction. In "Angels Passing," for instance, she describes how she spent an entire Christmas Eve "staring fixedly at Missy, [her] Pekingese, for hours, because a granny-woman had told [her] that God speaks through animals on Christmas Eve" (*Dimestore* 186). This anecdote nicely suggests the complicated intersection of religion and the sort of elemental, unrefined spirituality that often appears in Smith's work. Young Lee Smith presumably sought communication with the Christian God but did so by consulting a granny and a housecat rather than her family's pastor. In Smith's fiction from the 1990s she mines the friction, particularly within mountain families, between Christian doctrine and local custom, and the complexities of sexuality and family that that friction exposes.

In *The Devil's Dream, Saving Grace,* and *The Christmas Letters,* Smith also provides a more nuanced examination of community and social class than she does in the first decade of her career. While Smith's first novels described young women's feelings of restriction and repression by societal norms, her later novels take a long view of class issues, examining consequences for characters of all ages. In general, characters that follow their inclinations with little regard for community censure are disorganized and financially insecure. They tend, though, to be happier and more sexually satisfied than their counterparts who are consumed with proper appearances. However, most characters from Smith's 1990s fiction are not static in their approaches to balancing self and society. In *The Christmas Letters,* for instance, Mary Copeland's earliest letters are full of omissions and elisions. She lightheartedly thanks her neighbor Gerald Ruffin for a "real education" in one, without revealing her romantic feelings for him (52). Eventually, though, Mary divorces her wealthy husband Sandy, takes classes at the local college, and finds a supportive community of female friends, joining the Peace Corps in her fifties. In her life and her letters Mary grows more assured and fulfilled as she ages, pursuing and revealing her interests. Gender dynamics, as in Smith's treatment of religion, are a major influence on characters' choices and behavior. For years Sandy Copeland can, and does, get away with what Mary Copeland never thought she could.

As she examines characters' motivations for and machinations of keeping up appearances in their communities, Smith often brings mental illness into play. Much as Smith addressed religious issues without prominently featuring them prior to 1988s *Fair and Tender Ladies,* she began to write more frequently of mental illness in the 1990s. At least one character in each of the books discussed in this chapter struggles with an illness, whether that is addiction, depression, or anxiety. In two of her next three novels Smith intensifies this focus, building narratives with mental illness as their central concern.

Religion and Sexuality

With the short story "Tongues of Fire," first published in 1990 in *Me and My Baby View the Eclipse,* Smith signaled her intensified interest in religion as a driver of narrative. The story, set in 1957, is told by the adult woman Karen, who recounts her teenage conversion to backwoods Christianity. Karen turns to a rural church as her father has a "nervous breakdown" and her mother pretends that all is well (72). Like Crystal Spangler in *Black Mountain Breakdown* and Ivy Rowe in *Fair and Tender Ladies,* Karen is enticed by a charismatic preacher with a movie star name: Johnny Rock Malone. "It was a wipeout," she recalls; "I felt as fluttery and wild as could be" (81). Unlike Smith's earlier protagonists, though, Karen continues to crave God's presence long after the rush of her teenage feelings has abated. "I catch myself still listening for that voice," she confesses. "'Karen,' He will say, and I'll say, 'Yes, Lord. Yes'" (116). "Tongues of Fire" is an instructive bridge between Smith's fiction of the 1980s and 1990s. Karen's Christianity is more durable than that of any earlier protagonists in Smith's fiction, but not as strong as Grace Shepherd's would be in 1995s *Saving Grace.* Karen is also a relatively contemporary character. Smith's 1990s fiction is often set in the mid- to late-twentieth century rather than the distant mountain past of the 1980s novels such as *Oral History* and, to some degree, *Fair and Tender Ladies.*

From her first novel forward Smith's characters have navigated the sometimes blurry distinction between religious ecstasy and sexual passion. With religion's increased prominence in her 1990s works, this distinction also comes up in characters' lives more frequently. Questions of women's agency and familial love and lust accompany it; over and over in the works discussed here men dominate women in the name of Jesus, and brothers and sisters share uncomfortably close bonds. Nowhere are all of these religious issues more present than in Smith's most Christian-centric work, *Saving Grace.* In that novel Florida Grace Shepherd is raised by Virgil, her wild and unstable evangelist father, and Fannie, her loving, but tormented mother; she leaves the Pentecostal faith of her childhood as a young woman, only to return to it years later.

Grace has three significant sexual partners over the course of her story and conflates her sexual and religious experiences in her relationships with each of the three. Grace's vindictive half-brother Lamar is her first lover. Discussing her loss of her virginity to him at a church revival, the critic Conrad Ostwalt describes how Grace "gets swept away by the emotionally charged event, and finds herself in the backseat of her father's car with Lamar, transferring the 'butterflies' in her stomach and 'the general fever of that night' into sexual passion" (110). Grace makes the connection between religion and sex even more literal years later, after she begins an affair with Randy Newhouse: "I thought I had been born again" (225). In each of these relationships Grace draws the comparison between religious and sexual encounter. In her marriage to the somber pastor Travis Word, though, he is the partner who makes the comparison; he is consumed by religious guilt and shame every time he has sex with Grace. After their first time Travis begs Grace to pray with him. "Nothing would satisfy him," Grace recalls, "but for me to get down then and there on my knees too, both of us buck naked, as he quoted from Romans about our sinful passions working in our members to bear fruit for death. He was attempting to purify us" (188). Even after conceiving three children with Grace, Travis, as Linda Byrd Cook argues, "views the human body as symbol of imperfection, corruption, and base physicality" (170). For Grace, then, sex is tied up with two very different facets of Christianity: the exhilaration of revival and the shame and penitence of sin.

While Grace is thrilled by Lamar at the moment of their coupling, her half-brother is an immensely damaging presence in her life. In addition to Grace, Lamar seduces Grace's mother Fannie and Billie Jean, Grace's shy sister, in an effort to hurt Virgil. Fannie commits suicide as a result of their affair, and Billie Jean eventually is institutionalized after bearing Lamar's child. While the amount of hurt Lamar inflicts is striking, his role as a brother uncomfortably close to his sister is not unique in Smith's fiction. Female characters are infatuated with brothers or brother figures in *Fair and Tender Ladies, The Devil's Dream,* and *The Last Girls,* as well as in "The Bubba Stories" and "Live Bottomless" (both from *News of the Spirit*). This motif, as critic Martha Billips observes, is characterized by a "vulnerable young girl seduced (or raped) by a slightly older brother or brother figure" (129). Though these brother figures are not always aggressive or even aware of their sister's interest, Smith's inclusion of them suggests sexual disruption in the domestic sphere.

In her 2012 article "Siblings and Sex: A New Approach to the Fiction of Lee Smith," Billips thoroughly outlines the concerns that these inappropriate sibling relationships raise: "What at first might seem like consensual and lateral relationships actually display significant imbalances in power. The male in each case benefits from the prerogative of travel, and autonomy available to him in a patriarchal culture: he has more knowledge of the world than his 'sister,' and more sexual experience, and he is slightly older. The relationships also necessitate secrecy, something the 'brother' either enforces or the 'sister' instinctively grasps. . . . While Smith's characters from the 1990's may not recognize fully the problematic nature of their 'love' affairs, Smith clearly does, and she traces with increasing subtlety the consequences that these early relationships hold for the young girls involved and the adult women they become" (130).

Billips's analysis is particularly applicable to Grace and Lamar, as well as to Rose Annie and her older, nonbiological cousin Johnny Rainette in *The Devil's Dream*. Fragile Rose Annie calls Johnny "cousin, brother, heart of my heart, best friend" and is drawn to him from the time she learns to talk (136). The pair begins a sexual affair as teenagers, and though Rose Annie goes on to marry and have children with another man, she never stops thinking about Johnny. She remains infatuated, but even Rose Annie realizes some of the damage her relationship has caused her. As Billips observes, "Recounting a particularly risky sexual encounter the two have in close proximity to their gathered family and friends, Rose Annie acknowledges that 'something broke in me that night, and it has not gone back right ever since'" (145). Rose Annie and Johnny eventually marry and become famous singers in Nashville—her former mother-in-law calls her the Queen of Country Music—but their relationship remains toxic. When Johnny impregnates one of his many mistresses, the imbalance in the cousins' pairing irrevocably catches up to them: Rose Annie shoots her cheating husband dead and is confined to prison as a result.

The complications of sexual sibling relationships in Smith's fiction are generally negative, but in "The Bubba Stories" and "Live Bottomless" similar relationships are mined for poignant humor instead of outright tragedy. In "The Bubba Stories," from *News of the Spirit*, Charlene Christian invents a rakish brother to impress new friends at a Virginia women's college. "I was a little bit in love with him myself," Charlene admits (2). Bubba fits the archetype of Smith's brother characters: he is older than Charlene, often in trouble with authorities, and devilishly handsome. However, the important distinction between Bubba and other brother figures—that he is a fantasy of Charlene's own creation, within her control, and without a physical body—makes his presence amusing and, for Charlene, oddly helpful. Telling "the Bubba Stories" eases her anxiety about making friends and allows her to work out her sadness over the disappearance, in Vietnam, of a high school boyfriend. Charlene "kills" Bubba after she has an affair with a professor; she believes her own life has become sufficiently interesting. While Charlene never confesses the truth about Bubba to her friends, her relationships do not seem to suffer.

In *News of the Spirit's* "Live Bottomless," thirteen-year-old Jenny Dale fixates on her handsome brother-in-law Tom Burlington, the husband of her older sister. Like Charlene and Bubba's relationship, Jenny's intense crush on Tom is a coming-of-age kind of learning experience rather than a traumatic occurrence, but Jenny's infatuation is truer and sadder. "I loved Tom with a rapt, fierce, patient love," Jenny recalls. "Sometimes, I even talked myself into believing . . . that Tom had married Caroline only to get closer to *me,* to wait for me to grow up" (79). Tom initially indulges Jenny's crush in a relatively harmless way, reciting poetry to her and serving her a glass of champagne at his wedding. When he becomes a father, though, Tom is too distracted and uncomfortable to grant time to Jenny. "I had *grown up,* I felt. I had been tongue-kissed, and lived among stars. I was ready for him," she says. "But when they arrived, Tom wouldn't pay a bit of attention to me. . . . All he would do was wait on Caroline . . . and make goo-goo eyes at his stupid little pointy-headed baby" (151). Jenny talks him into a tour of Key West while they are on a family trip there, but he agrees reluctantly and continually suggests that they return to the hotel.

The contrast between Jenny's pride in her increased sophistication and Tom's disinterest hurts Jenny's feelings, but it also creates a defining moment for her, a bittersweet moment of recognition and actual maturity. Jenny runs from him in the middle of Key West; he angrily calls her a "little bitch" when he catches up to her. "What a relief!" she thinks. "I have been recognized at last. I *am* a little bitch, and I will never be an angel, and it's okay. I start laughing, and Tom starts laughing, too" (154). A "street photographer" captures the pair with "arms wound tightly around each other . . . look[ing] like lovers" (155). Though Jenny loses touch with Tom, who later leaves his family to pursue another woman, she carries the photo with her for decades. "For some reason," she says, "I can't quit writing this story, or looking at this picture, in which the sun is so bright, and Tom Burlington and I are smiling like crazy. I guess it reminds me of Mama and Daddy in love." (156). Jenny moves on from her fantasy of Tom and, more generally, survives a turning point in her idealistic youth. "I will learn," Jenny says. "And I will get my period, and some breasts. . . . I will never be really good again" (155).

While Smith's sexual brother-sister relationships are almost always about control, that control is not always tied to religion. Smith features a striking number of other relationships, though—some sexual, some not—in which men cite Christian doctrine as justification for controlling girls and women. In *The Devil's Dream,* for instance, the conflict between old-time religion and good-time music is central along the Bailey family's path to Nashville fame. Beginning in the 1830s with Kate Malone, the daughter of a fiddler, who marries Moses Bailey, the son of a primitive Baptist preacher, women find their behavior and artistry restricted in the name of God. "Moses wouldn't hardly let her go back" to visit her family after the marriage, according to Ira Keen, the couple's former neighbor. "He said that the Devil walked in that house, and that fiddle music was the voice of the Devil laughing" (23). When Kate defies him by sneaking a fiddle into the house to play with their son Jeremiah, Moses becomes violent. "One side of Kate's pretty face was black and blue," Ira says, "and her eye was swole shut" (29). Jeremiah suffers worse; sent away by Moses, he falls down a rocky section of mountain and is killed; Moses dies soon after and Kate goes mad. Women and children are both at the mercy of fathers and dogma in *The Devil's Dream,* but some children adopt their parents' strict religion rather than softening it. Ezekiel "Zeke" Bailey, for instance, another child of Kate and Moses, forbids his wife and daughter from attending a medicine show for reasons that echo his father's. Zeke asks Nonnie, his wife "why in the world she would want to go see something like that, and mentioned that God was against it, for it had been so preached from the pulpit Sunday past" (71). Like her mother-in-law Kate, Nonnie defies her husband, and, as for Kate, the results are tragic: Nonnie leaves town with the medicine show and dies in a hotel fire three years later.

Men also are violent and controlling in the name of religion in *Saving Grace.* Virgil Shepherd's belief in pain and danger as an expression of faith carries over to his treatment of his family. He is said to have survived more than two hundred snakebites, and he occasionally drinks poison and fasts. Because of his control over his family, Grace, her siblings, and her mother often suffer along with Virgil. As a child, for instance, Grace opposes Virgil by helping her younger brother get medical treatment instead of faith healing. "Daddy . . . whipped me with his belt until I bled," Grace recalls (64). Grace internalizes her father's rules, hiding the fact that she can drive a car from him because she knows, without his saying, that it will upset him. "I did not want to displease Daddy," she says, "for he was a real power in those days, and I could not have gone against him" (137). The degree to which Virgil has nearly unbreakable control over Grace is evident after the death of her mother, Fannie. In spite of Virgil's role in Fannie's suicide, his imprisonment, and his increasingly erratic behavior, Grace never leaves Virgil. Instead he and his wild girlfriend Carlean run away together, abandoning Grace in a rundown trailer.

Virgil has conditioned Grace to accept the control of pastors and preachers to such an extent that Grace moves in with Travis Word and his sister Helen immediately after her father leaves. Though Travis is in many ways a good and kind husband, and his sister a supportive helper, their attitudes toward pleasure show how piety can manifest as misogyny and control. At Grace's wedding, for instance, Helen tells the baker to write "'Glory to God Amen'" on the wedding cake instead of "'Travis and Gracie in Love.'" The "other was too undignified for a preacher," Helen tells Grace, and Grace, used to being led, agrees (181). After the wedding, Travis provides his wife with a home and stability, but he also marshals Christian doctrine to restrict Grace's choices and stem her sexual desires. "I had to kneel down there and pray, too" after sex, Grace recalls. "After a while, I got to where I did not often try to tempt him, as it was not really worth it" (197).

Helen does not directly influence the couple's sex life, but she invokes God when she chooses Grace's clothes, prepares the family's food, and tries to name the couple's first child. A recent widow, she performs nearly all the duties that Grace would otherwise assume as Travis's wife. "Helen Tate had always filled that role herself," Grace says, "and continued to; . . . I got out of all that" (190). While there is no indication that Travis and Helen have any sort of sexual relationship, her role in Grace and Travis's marriage is unusual and stifling; with no tasks to complete or roles to fill Grace feels "idle and restless" and "like a bird in a nest" (190). Helen displaces Grace and remains with Travis long after he and Grace have divorced; she continues to exert control over Grace by withholding her mail and restricting access to her children.

As Helen's actions suggest, the limits that Christian characters place on behavior and artistry in Smith's novels are not only imposed by men. Generations after Kate Malone's struggle, her great-great-granddaughter Katie Cocker encounters religious-based opposition to her music from her mother Alice Bailey. Alice, according to Katie, "said flat-out that there was *no way* she was going to ever consent to me trying to be a singer, . . . for she was convinced that most singing was a sin" (211). The difference between Moses Bailey's restrictions and Alice Bailey's, though, is that Moses seeks to control his wife, while Alice's impulse is to keep and protect her daughter. Unlike most of her aunts, uncles, and cousins, Alice does not perform as a musician. As a girl she feels special when she is allowed to go with relatives to listen to a Grand Ole Opry radio broadcast: "I felt like a part of my family too, and a part of that music they loved so. See, they always left us behind when they went off someplace to sing. I didn't hardly know Mamma at all" (115). Reserved by nature, Alice usually feels that music further marginalizes her and keeps her from connecting with her family; she does not want to lose her daughter to it. By turning to Christianity, Alice gains access to a church community in which she fits in, and she also gains a framework for dealing with a world of which she is scared. "Honey, you don't know what's out there," she tells Katie when her daughter goes on the road as a performer. "Out in the world . . . you just don't know, honey, what all a girl can get into" (214). Alice has been wounded by her abusive alcoholic husband and remains terrified of physical contact.

Katie eventually embraces Christianity herself, but she believes that she resisted it for so long because of Alice. As Tanya Long Bennett observes, "Katie's religion is different from her mother's. It is a more primary experience than Alice's seems to be" (Bennett "It was like I was right there" 91). Katie's conversion is an intensely sensual moment that is rooted in the bodily pleasures of which Alice is so wary. "I could feel my pain rushing up from all over my body," she says, "feel the shock when it hit the air, feel it shatter and blow away. . . . Then I felt God come into me, right into me through the mouth, like a long cool drink of water" (298). While Alice's faith is based on abstinence and restraint, Katie's is almost decadent. "What my God says to me is *Yes! Yes!*," Katie says, "instead of *No! No!* which is all God ever said to anybody up on Chicken Rise" (298). Although her joy is refreshing, Smith cannily suggests that Katie's enabling variety of Christianity is due in part to her celebrity as a country-music artist. After the death of her true love, Ralph Handy, Katie is approached by a minister named Billy Jack Reems. Billy Jack promises relief from her pain, and, soon, Katie is attending the "Hallelujah Congregation" with "a lot of us in the music business." Katie's sense of peace in the church is real, but so is the money she and her fellow artists donate to move the church from a YMCA into a "new Building for Celebration" (298).

While dogmatic Christianity is so often presented as a negative force in Smith's fiction, she explores a womanist alternative to it at moments in *Saving Grace*. If Virgil represents a faith built upon suffering, danger, and violence, Grace's mother Fannie shows the way to a kinder, more joyful way of belief. "She was always happy and singing," Grace recalls, "church songs mostly" (26). Fannie's doctrine is accompanied by physical warmth, which comforts her children when they are uncertain about their father's actions. When she speaks to Grace of God, Fannie shows her daughter the emotional and physical affection her father never does: "'The Lord will provide,'" she tells Grace, "smoothing [her] long yellow hair and pressing [her] against her bosom" (3).

Fannie's execution of her faith is far from perfect; her continued devotion to Virgil keeps her from being an effective advocate for her children, as does her absence when she commits suicide after sleeping with Lamar. She enforces her husband's will when called upon, lifting a heavy cooking dish to strike her oldest son when he defies Virgil.

Still, it is through her mother that Grace, even after such awful experiences, ultimately returns to Christianity. At thirty-seven, in the midst of her second divorce, Grace returns to her childhood home at Scrabble Creek, seeking communion with God through Fannie. The critic Debra Druesedow describes her journey: "She is drawn to the place of her childhood to remember, to reflect, to find what she has been missing to tell; thus, the narrative circles back to the frame and to the present" (77). At the family's old house she sleeps in her mother's bed before donning one of Fannie's old dresses. Suddenly Grace feels the presence of God in the same way that Fannie did: "I will let my hands do what they are drawing now to do and it does not hurt, it is a joy in the Lord as she said. It is a joy which spreads all through my body, all through this sinful old body of mine" (271). The "she" whom Grace mentions is, of course, Fannie, whom she is emulating by grasping hot coals from the woodstove in her hands. By adopting her mother's behavior in her childhood home, Grace, as the critic Joan Wylie Hall has written, "'knows' herself because mother and daughter, past and present, heaven and earth are miraculously united" (85). Rebecca Smith puts it more concretely when she argues that, in *Saving Grace,* Smith "create[s] female characters who can move beyond the constraints imposed by a patriarchal society and a patriarchal religion, who can find identity and spiritual fulfillment because God speaks to them in an feminine voice" (11).

Community and Appearances

Much as religion often restricts characters in Smith's 1990's fiction, upper-middle-class white communities impose limits and controls in these novels and stories. While social class has been a concern in Smith's fiction since the beginning of her career, Smith's 1990s fiction addresses it most frequently in contemporary settings. Issues of class affect the choices Smith's characters make about everything from religion to friendship and sexuality. Though characters of all ages are susceptible to its pressures, teenagers, such as Karen of "Tongues of Fire" in *Me and My Baby View the Eclipse,* are disproportionately affected; in that story Karen's parents simply discourage socialization with members of certain socioeconomic groups. In Smith's work the desire to cross social boundaries exists in both directions: the daughters of ladylike mothers are excited to try canned stew at their friend's modest houses, and the daughters of poor parents are curious about the country club.

Karen memorably lays out the connection between class and religion when she relates her mother's guidelines for church attendance. She says: "My mother had already explained to me the social ranking of the churches: Methodist at the top, attended by doctors and lawyers and other 'nice' families; Presbyterian slightly down the scale, attended by store owners; then the vigorous Baptists; then the Church of Christ, who thought they were the only real church in town and said so. . . . And then, of course, at the *very bottom* of the church scale were those little churches out in the surrounding county, some of them recognizable denominations (Primitive Baptist) and some of them not (Church of the Nazarene, Tar River Holiness) where people were reputed to yell out, fall down in fits, and throw their babies" (64).

In her explanation Karen's mother echoes Brooke Kincaid's mother Carolyn in *Something in the Wind,* who marvels that her friend is a Baptist. "Nobody in the world is a Baptist except the lower elements and the Hugheses" (14). Unlike Brooke, however, Karen quickly and purposefully inserts herself into the "very bottom" of her mother's denominational ranking system. When she finds out that her friend Tammy's mother attends a rural church where she speaks in tongues, Karen draws on class distinctions to gain admission to that church. "I would get to go to church with Tammy and her mother," she relates; "in return, I would take Tammy to the country club" (88). Karen's attendance at Tammy's church is so transgressive to her mother that she sends her daughter to an extended summer camp with class-appropriate Episcopal services. Though Karen once speaks in tongues at camp, her mother's actions have their desired effects. She never goes back to Tammy's house after her return, and she goes on to "make cheerleader," "go to college," "get breasts," and "have babies" (116). When Karen stops crossing religious boundaries, she adopts behaviors more conventional of her social class, too.

Grace, like Karen's friend Tammy, longs to cross socioeconomic boundaries in the opposite direction: she frequently is resentful of the monetary and cultural hardships that her father's faith imposes on her family. At school Grace recalls being "embarrassed about my own lunch, which was nothing but a piece of cornbread usually, and sometimes a mason jar of buttermilk to break the cornbread up in. . . . Some days I didn't have a lunch at all, and then I always said I was on a diet" (44). The poverty that Grace tries to hide is directly traceable to her family's religious beliefs. As an adult Grace sometimes chafes against Travis Word's monetary philosophy. On the day of their wedding, for instance, she is disappointed to find that Travis plans to take her back to his house for the night. "'When I got to thinking about it,'" he tells Grace, "'it just seemed to me like a sinful waste of money to spend twenty dollars on a motel room when we have got our own bed at home'" (183). Travis's guilt about spending money is connected with his guilt about having sex with Grace, a link that the motel-room conversation pointedly illustrates. For much of Grace's life Christianity means material deprivation and sometimes emotional humiliation.

Grace's family's religious identification also isolates them within their community. Despite the rotating masses of religious followers Virgil attracts, Grace rightly feels that many parts of mainstream society are inaccessible to her. After visiting her friend Marie Royal, when Marie's grandparents call, Grace thinks, "I didn't know my own grandparents—I didn't even know if I had any. We didn't have a telephone at our house either" (53). Ultimately, Grace's family also cuts off her connection with Marie: when her friend unexpectedly drops by the house on Scrabble Creek, she sees Virgil and Grace's brother Joe covered in blood after a violent fight. "Marie started crying. . . . Her mother got out of the car and started screaming for her to come. Without a word to [Grace], Marie turned and ran down the hill and got in the car, and then they were gone" (64). Though Marie's family has been kind to and supportive of Grace despite what they know of her parents, they stop associating with her once Marie is put into a potentially dangerous situation. Unlike the middle-class families in many of Smith's novels, the Shepherds have little interest in keeping up appearances or upholding community standards, unless they are related to God.

Perhaps even more so than religion, romantic relationships are closely linked to status in Smith's 1990s fiction; characters often find freedom in new partnerships that affect their class or community position. In, for instance, "The Southern Cross," from *News of the Spirit* Mayruth "Chanel" Keen pursues a married man in an attempt to leave her poor eastern Kentucky upbringing behind. For much of her story Chanel relates the shallow lessons she's learned about using taste and appearance to cross class boundaries. "I wouldn't eat another soup bean if my life depended on it," she says. "Give me caviar. Which I admit I did not take to at first as it is so salty, but . . . there are some things you just have to like if you want to rise up in the world" (158). In addition to eating expensive foods, Chanel plans to begin wearing hair bows like the wealthy Atlanta wives she envies (158). "'Bowheads is what I call them, all those Susans and Ashleys and Elizabeths" (161). It doesn't matter to Chanel that she doesn't especially like the caviar or the bows, which she calls "embarrassing"; social mobility by way of shallow signifiers is her primary concern.

On a trip to the Caribbean, though, Chanel begins to realize the value of personal authenticity. Prompted by the drunken mistreatment of her married "fiancé" and his wealthy friend on a yacht, Chanel "all of a sudden" decides she "just can't do it" and flees the boat in a dinghy. "I use the rowing machine all the time at the health club," she thinks, "but this is the first time I have had a chance at the real thing" (174). Previously uninterested in constellations or the local musician who seems attracted to her, Chanel changes her mind and plans to go "native," admiring Orion's belt as she rows under a "whole damn sky [full] of stars." "A part of me can't believe I'm acting this crazy," she says, "while another part of me is saying, 'Go, girl'" (175).

Another woman who is fulfilled when a change in her relationship leads to a change in her social class is Mary Copeland of *The Christmas Letters*. The second narrator of the novella, Mary goes from living on a modest farm to living in a wealthy suburban neighborhood as her husband advances in his career. She initially upholds the conventions of her middle-class community in her Christmas letters. "I want everybody out there to know that I am *fine*, happy as can be in this little aqua shoebox of a home with my baby Andrew" (46). Mary is comfortable using her community's discourse and knows what she ought to reveal in polite letters.

It is only later in the novella, once Mary and her husband Sandy have divorced, that Mary writes an honest Christmas letter. Addressing only her

"Very Special Friends," Mary writes "*A Real Christmas Letter, the First Ever*," acknowledging that her others have been deceptively incomplete (83). While she lived in the "aqua shoebox," for instance, Mary actually was having an emotional affair with her neighbor, the alcoholic Gerald Ruffin. "We used to sit out on those crummy lawn chairs talking and talking all night long," she writes, " . . . while the bugs flew around and the Big Al's Tire sign shone all night long just beyond the blooming honeysuckle that covered the stockade fence enclosing us from the 'bad neighborhood,' which surrounded us on every side. Oh, how sweet that honeysuckle smelled—I will never forget it" (91). Without her former upper-middle-class friends as an audience, Mary is free to tell her life's story as she truly sees it.

When Mary stops abiding by her sense of obligation to Sandy and their community, she is amazed at the life she creates. Just as her letters become more honest, so too do her actions: Mary attends college, accepts her gay son's boyfriend as more than just "a friend from California" (82), and even joins the Peace Corps. The food references that close the last two Christmas letters of the novella nicely illustrate Mary's new freedom. In the former of these letters Mary writes that her son and his boyfriend are carrying on the family's tradition of making "Sticks and Stones" for Christmas (118). The recipe, which is hand-me-down from Mary's mother Birdie, has always been Mary's responsibility to prepare. In her post-divorce life, however, Mary is willing to delegate responsibility and to be cared for in addition to caring for others. The second recipe, which is the last in the novella, is one that Mary sends from her Peace Corps post in Africa. "Ndiwoz Az Mpiru Wotendera" contains greens and peanut butter and is shared by Mary's daughter Melanie in her first Christmas letter. "I almost forgot this recipe from Mom," Melanie writes, "(who said not to mention the anthropologist)" (126). The recipes together trace a lineage of female support from Birdie to Mary to Melanie that each woman values. By the end of her story Mary has learned to balance family with her own inclinations and tradition with new experiences.

When men experience status change through relationships in Smith's fiction, it is often because they are leaving prim wives for messier but more emotionally open or artistically expressive women. In "Intensive Care" in *Me and My Baby View the Eclipse*, Harold Stikes "deserted his lovely wife and three children" for Cherry, "a redheaded waitress"—a fallen woman with a checkered past," much to the consternation of the beauty parlor and the "lovely wife" Joan (162). Yet Harold is happier than ever, despite Cherry's terminal illness. "He loves his wife. He feels that he has been ennobled and enlarged, by knowing Cherry Oxendine. . . . He stepped out of his average life for her, he gave up being a good man, but the rewards have been extraordinary" (188). Harold's change is so momentous that it prompts otherworldly recognition. Thinking on his good fortune, Harold happens upon a UFO. "Although Harold can't say exactly how it communicates to him or even if it does, suddenly his soul is filled to bursting. The ineffable occurs" (188).

The same sort of upper-class malaise that emboldens Harold to pursue Cherry leads other characters in Smith's 1990s fiction to develop or display worsening anxiety, depression, or addiction. Yet, because of the importance of "keeping up appearances," these problems are almost never addressed by characters in clinical terms or disclosed to their children. For many of the youngest narrators in Smith's fiction—Karen, who is thirteen years old in "Tongues of Fire," for instance—these sidesteps mean that the mental illness of a parent can be liberating instead of just disconcerting. With her family distracted by her father's depression, Karen has greater autonomy to venture to her friend Tammy's rural home. She is also, for better and worse, free to imagine how her father feels and what the potential outcomes of his situation could be; no one tells her what to expect.

In their study of the nervous breakdown in twentieth-century American culture, the social historians Megan Barke, Rebecca Fribush, and Peter N. Stearns note the appeal of the term *nervous breakdown* in discourse communities. "In an age of medicalization," they explain, "people liked the idea of a disease entity that described symptoms and anxieties they felt, rather than an entity clearly delimited by the burgeoning apparatus of the mental health professionals" (566). The term also came into popular usage because it remained essentially undefined: "Flexible vagueness made it a valid catchall" for any number of issues (576). The term's vagueness comes in handy for parents in Smith's novels. After Karen's mother says to her, "your father is having a nervous breakdown," she declines to elaborate. "This was the only time," Karen thinks, "she ever mentioned my father's nervous breakdown out loud, in her whole life" (*Me and My Baby* 72). By telling family and friends only that her husband had a nervous breakdown, Karen's mother Dee can admit that he has a problem without confirming any of its potentially embarrassing symptoms.

Without further clarification from her mother, Karen is left to puzzle out the meaning of her father's "nervous breakdown" on her own. Initially, her appraisal of his condition is limited. "This explained the way my father's eye twitched and watered now, behind his gold-rimmed glasses," she thinks; "[he] spent more time lying on the daybed upstairs in his study, holding books or magazines in his hands but not reading them" (*Me and My Baby* 73). What Karen does understand, instead of her father's experience, is her mother's unstated plan for dealing with it.

1. The husband *should not* have a nervous breakdown.
2. Nobody can mention the nervous breakdown. It is shameful.
3. The children must *behave* at all times during the nervous breakdown.
4. The family must keep up appearances at all costs. Nobody should know.
    (*Me and My Baby* 72)

It is only when Karen's father collapses in tears on the golf course that she realizes mental illness is more than a supposed source of shame. "I had come realize somehow, during the course of that afternoon" she recalls, "that . . . we might never be all right again" (*Me and My Baby* 92).

Karen becomes interested in speaking in tongues just a few days after her father's collapse, looking, as Ostwalt argues, for a measure of control. "The first time Karen hears glossolalia, she knows she has discovered a source of power at her friend's Holiness church" (112). Though she does not understand her mother's vague language at home, Karen immediately connects with the strange sounds she hears in church. It is, she thinks, "a language which I felt I knew intimately, somehow, better than I knew English. It was *my language*" (*Me and My Baby* 96). Though Karen claims familiarity and ownership of the words she hears—and, later, speaks—she values the attention the words command, too. At summer camp, when Karen believes God appears to her alone in a cabin, she recalls how she immediately knew what to do. "I . . . washed my face and brushed my teeth, . . . tucked in my shirt, and ran up the hill to the assembly hall," Karen says. "I opened my mouth, closed my eyes, and started speaking in Tongues of Fire" (*Me and My Baby* 111). It is important for Karen to be in front of an audience when she speaks, and she takes the time to groom herself before she does so. Though there is an evangelical explanation for Karen's choice to speak in the assembly hall, it is clear that she is also just eager to be heard, even when speaking words her peers do not understand.

Nervous breakdowns in Smith's fiction sometimes are accompanied by or conflated with alcoholism. In "Live Bottomless," for instance, Jenny's mother Billie enters treatment—"'a nice little rest,'" as adults describe it to Jennifer—after her appetite for gin and tonics gets out of hand (*News of the Spirit* 95). Worsened by the death of her younger brother and the discovery of her husband's affair, Billie's reliance on alcohol is a symptom of her larger psychological struggles. Alcoholism also is at the forefront of *The Devil's Dream,* where it is addressed more explicitly. Katie Cocker knows from a young age that her grandfather Durwood and her father drink too much, despite her mother's attempts to keep that information from her. "Tillie Dew said her mamma said that my granddaddy was an alcoholic," Katie tells Alice after riding the school bus one day. Alice's response is more violent than those of Karen's mother or

Jenny's father. "She slapped me so far across the face that I fell against the wall," Katie recalls (220). Even in the rural Grassy Branch community, addiction is stigmatized and supposed to remain a sort of open secret.

Though Katie eventually begins drinking too much herself, her openness about alcoholism and her other struggles suggests that she mostly has healed. Katie accepts her failings instead of hiding them, and, as the name of her section of the novel suggests, "tells it like it is" (207). In her openness about addiction and treatment, Katie is one of a handful of characters in Smith's 1990s fiction to address directly, as narrator, her own mental illness. In works to follow, particularly 2013's *Guests on Earth*, Smith features more perspectives like Katie's, letting the ill speak for themselves: appearances be damned.

CHAPTER 6

I Have Lived in the Fire for Years, Yet Here I Am

Family Linen, The Last Girls, and Guests on Earth

Nearly twenty years separate the publication of *Family Linen* (1985) from that of *The Last Girls* (2002), and the latter of those works came ten years before *Guests on Earth* (2013). Drawn as they are, however, from three different decades of Lee Smith's writing life, these novels share a thematic and tonal approach. Each is concerned with often-interconnected issues of mental illness and memory and the impacts those issues have on familial and friendly relationships. Smith grapples with this subject matter by employing what she has called "onlooker" narratives. Narrators such as Sybill Hess (*Family Linen*), Harriet Holding (*The Last Girls*), and Evalina Toussaint (*Guests on Earth*) do not see themselves as characters worthy of narrative focus. Instead each woman positions herself as a teller of tales about a more interesting person. From *Family Linen* to *Guests on Earth*, Smith puts increasing physical and temporal distance between her narrators and their supposed subjects; while Sybill, whose story Smith tells in the limited third-person, fixates on her mother's past, Evalina provides her first-person impressions of Zelda Fitzgerald, with whom she was institutionalized in the 1940s.

Smith's authorial interest in mental illness has roots in her personal life. In *Dimestore* she describes her father's bipolar disorder and lists half a dozen members of her mother's family who were, at one point or another, mentally ill. Her family's difficulties led Smith to question her own sanity, particularly as a young woman. "I grew up to some degree feeling that if you didn't fit right in, if you didn't conform, you would go crazy," she told Virginia Smith. Though her worries went mostly unfounded—"I have been oddly sane," she says—Smith's son Joshua Seay struggled with disorders from his teenage years until his death at age thirty-three (Tate 72). Smith recently has written about how his hospitalization in Highland Hospital, where Zelda Fitzgerald was treated periodically from 1936 until her death in 1948, directly compelled her to write *Guests on Earth*. "I remember the exact moment when I realized I was going to write this book," she recalled in the essay 'In Her Words'. "My son and I were walking up Zillicoa Avenue toward the mountain-top hospital during a particularly brilliant winter sunset." Reminded of the fire that damaged Highland and killed Fitzgerald, Smith also thought about physical and emotional entrapment, particularly as they related, respectively, to the hospital building and Zelda's exasperation with her husband's possessiveness.

From *Family Linen* to *Guests on Earth*, Smith's onlooker narrators move progressively closer, in terms of both physical space and emotional intimacy, to mentally ill characters. In *Family Linen*, for instance, most of the titular family easily avoids Fay, who secludes herself in a dark room and has only limited mobility. In *The Last Girls*, however, Harriet shares a small dorm room with Baby, who also is her best friend. When Baby unsuccessfully attempts suicide, it is Harriet who finds her; when, years later, Baby dies in mysterious circumstances, it is Harriet who agonizes over Baby's unknowable intentions and mourns her friend. She, rather than Baby's widower, is the steward of her friend's ashes, charged with scattering them into the Mississippi. Still, when Baby is institutionalized, Harriet is not with her, and the girls never discuss Baby's treatment. Even Harriet's degree of distance from mental illness is eradicated in *Guests on Earth*. After witnessing her mother's severe postpartum depression, which ultimately results in her suicide, in the confined spaces of their shared home Evalina is sent to a mental hospital. At Highland Hospital she is intimately involved with the mentally ill during their periods of treatment and recovery. Her own categorization—sane or ill, part of the community or an outsider—remains murky, too, unclear both in her own mind and in the story Evalina tells.

Smith highlights the manipulation of memory as a means of institutional treatment for and personal response to mental illnesses in *Family Linen*, *The Last Girls*, and *Guests on Earth*. While Sybill sees a hypnotist and discovers that her persistent headaches are a result of traumatic repressed memories, Harriet rehashes her college memories in order to gain a sense of closure about the deaths of Baby and of Jeff Carr, the boy they both loved. Because Evalina, whose experiences with mental illness occur decades earlier in the twentieth century than those of Sybill and Harriet, is also the only main character in these novels who receives long-term intensive treatment for mental illness, her experiences are the most direct. Evalina undergoes convulsive shock therapy that clouds her memory and renders her own traumatic experiences inaccessible to her for weeks at a time. In each of these three novels Smith poses difficult questions about the value of memories: are troubling memories, for instance, more damaging when repressed or when excruciatingly accessible? To what extent can subjective memories—the only kind of memories—be trusted? And what are the consequences of the external manipulation of one's memory? Collectively, these novels suggest that remembering almost always is preferable to forgetting and that mysteries and loss are inevitable and must be accepted.

In many of Lee Smith's novels friendships between adult women have taken a narrative backseat to familial relationships. *Family Linen* conforms to this trend. In that novel Sybill is prompted to see a hypnotist by a female friend, but most of her fraught interactions in the novel are with family members, particularly her sister Candy. With *The Last Girls,* however, Smith made female friendship a focal point of the novel; while each character's family life is explored, the novel's structure and framing plot are determined by friendships. The same can be said for *Guests on Earth,* in which Evalina loses her biological family very early in the novel. Instead of probing the ways in which Evalina's mental illness impacts her family relationships, Smith creates a changeable community at Highland Hospital, which mostly is populated by women and girls. Evalina frequently thinks of her mother, but the women with whom she must navigate her daily life are friends such as Dixie, a Georgia beauty queen whose depression leads her in and out of Evalina's life, and wild Ella Jean Bascomb, the daughter of a hospital cook.

As in the rest of her oeuvre Smith's exploration of relationships is grounded in her concern with female subjectivity. This concern especially is evident in *The Last Girls* and *Guests on Earth,* in which Harriet and Evalina claim to subjugate their own narratives to those of other women with whom they are acquaintances or friends. Though the progressive, chronological trend in Smith's novels is from passive female characters toward more active, self-confident ones, the novels discussed in this chapter represent something of a regression, or qualification, in terms of the female main characters' agency. Instead of being juxtaposed with relatively fulfilled characters, such as Candy in *Family Linen,* Evalina and Harriet are paired in friendship with women whose creativity and passion are frustrated by societal censure and their own mental illnesses. For Harriet, Baby is both fascinating and tragic, while Evalina observes the highs and lows of Zelda Fitzgerald. The dichotomy that Smith has explored throughout her career is not as neat, *The Last Girls* and *Guests on Earth* suggest, as active or passive. Active women must defend their actions. Speaking of Zelda in *Guests on Earth,* a nurse observes: "None of them knew what to do with her. She was too smart, too or-i-gin-al. She was too wild and she drank too much and she didn't fit in. . . . And that's enough" (148). Smith does not advocate passivity as a lifestyle in these or any other of her novels, but she also does not pretend that a life of one's choosing is necessarily an easy one to navigate.

Although it is useful to highlight the similarities of these novels, they are different also in important ways. While, for instance, *Family Linen* and *The Last Girls* both employ multiple narrators, *Guests on Earth* is told solely from Evalina's point of view. Like many of Smith's recent novels, though, *Guests on Earth* includes an array of fictionalized historical sources. To create her narrative Evalina compiles postcards, letters, a newspaper clipping, and reproductions of pages from Zelda Fitzgerald's notebook, all of which appear as illustrations in the novel. *Guests on Earth* also is distinguished by its setting in the early twentieth century. The settings of both *Family Linen* and *The Last Girls*, the 1980s and 1990s, respectively, were mostly contemporary at the times of their publication. Structurally, each novel is fairly representative of the period in Smith's career during which it was produced. *Family Linen*'s arrangement recalls that of *Oral History*, while *The Last Girls* shares traits with those novels as well as with *The Christmas Letters*, which incorporates few sources besides its characters' varied voices.

While each of the novels discussed in this chapter was greeted by largely favorable reviews, *The Last Girls* received the most media attention. Featured by the *Good Morning America* Book Club, the novel became a *New York Times* bestseller and a co-winner of the Southern Book Critics Circle Award. Coverage of the novel frequently reveals fascination with its autobiographical shadings. Like Smith, the female protagonists attend a private Virginia women's college, and, more interestingly, they also construct a raft with classmates and pilot it down the Mississippi River. Smith and fifteen of her classmates did the same in the summer of 1966. *Publishers Weekly* called the novel a "reimagin[ing]" of Smith's own "prefeminist odyssey" and its aftermath, while Sarah Towers, writing in the *New York Times,* noted thematic overlap between Smith's authorial process and the novel's material. "Smith's desire to step back into old footprints dovetails with the theme of *The Last Girls*," she writes; "the book is about what it means to go back, to re-examine forgotten routes and narratives." Towers's analysis is particularly true of *The Last Girls,* but it also could be expanded to each of the three novels discussed here. (The *Publisher's Weekly* review was published July 1, 2002. The *New York Times* review is from October 6, 2002.)

Mental Illness

Mental illness is a central focus of *Family Linen, The Last Girls,* and *Guests on Earth*, but Smith has emphasized its presence and effects in nearly every novel and story collection she has published. *Black Mountain Breakdown,* for instance, could be included here for its attention to alcoholism and repression, as could short stories such as "Artists" (*Cakewalk*) for its portrayal of dementia. What sets these novels apart in their treatment of this subject is their pronounced focus on the acknowledgement and care of the mentally ill as diseased. For most of her life Crystal Spangler of *Black Mountain Breakdown* is treated as a normal, even "perfect," daughter who simply has a few odd moments of disconnection. Even in Crystal's catatonic state, her friend Agnes believes that she "might jump right up from that bed tomorrow and go off and get her Ph.D. or do something else crazy" (240). In *The Last Girls,* however, Baby Ballou's friends cannot pretend that their suicidal friend is not ill, no matter how good she may be at trying to convince them that she is not. Because of the open acknowledgement of disease in these novels, Smith is able to address its clinical consequences and feature characters discussing it more explicitly. Her narrative exploration progressively increases when these three novels are read in the order of their publication; mental illnesses take up more and more physical and narrative space.

In *Family Linen* illness is severe, with obvious physical consequences, but characters attempt to hide it behind evasive expressions and closed doors. While Sybill narrates much of the novel and personally experiences repression, the character in that novel whose illness is most damaging is Sybill's Aunt Fay. Secretly led on by her sister's husband and guilty of murdering him, Fay, years later, is housebound and lost in a world of TV soap operas and limited human contact. Alone with her secrets, Fay becomes a grotesque figure, enormous and incoherent in her claustrophobic den. She is "getting real heavy now," her nephew Arthur observes, "like a big white slug that never sees the light of day" (88). By describing Fay thusly, Smith invites comparisons of her to other figures in Southern fiction, especially Emily Grierson of Faulkner's "A Rose for Emily." Like Fay, Emily grows large and sequesters herself indoors for years at a time. Both women also kill their lovers when they threaten to leave. While Emily literally stays in bed with Homer Barron's body, Fay remains nearly immobile, occupied with Jewell Rife in her mind. As Terrell Tebbetts observes, "It is as if Fay entered the well with Jewell's body and has never climbed out" (105).

In her description of the Southern grotesque, the critic Sarah Gleeson-White could practically be writing a description of Fay. The trope, she argues, generally includes "freakish outsiders placed in lovelorn, barren landscapes, penetrating heat, and closed spaces, with themes of miscegenation, sexual deviance, and bloody violence" (108). The applicability of Gleeson-White's description to Fay is sadly underscored when Fay dies: "Miss Fay has gone and shut herself up in Clinus's old Chevrolet out there," the man who finds her body says. "It was the heat that killed her, it looks like" (254). Fay's rape by Jewell Rife leads her to increasingly claustrophobic spaces, the last of which is too much to survive.

Mental illness is packaged in a beautiful, less reclusive person in *The Last Girls*. Baby Ballou is young, wealthy, and smart, with a "slow but reckless toothy grin that no one could ever resist" (118). For long stretches of time she lives among other people; Baby dwells in dormitory rooms and fraternity parties instead of in a dank den like Fay's. In her case the illness, rather than the person whom it afflicts, is the thing hidden away. When Baby's struggle emerges, though, it is no less formidable. A seemingly half-hearted attempt at suicide—"You didn't really mean it then, right?" Harriet asks, reluctant as ever to acknowledge the seriousness of Baby's struggle. "Or you would have gone for the vein"—ends with Baby sitting in a bloody dorm bathtub, "her face dead white in the stark fluorescent light. She had black shadows like smudges under her eyes and no expression, none whatsoever, in them" (171). Perhaps because her illness and treatment have remained hidden, Harriet accepts Baby's request not to take her in for evaluation after this attempt. The fact that neither Fay nor Baby often receives professional care for her illness suggests the tendency to brush aside diseases of the mind rather than treat them, whether hidden or in plain sight.

By way of its sheer number of mentally ill characters, *Guests on Earth* is able to feature women like Fay and like Baby, along with types in between. If *Family Linen* highlighted the vulnerability of the poor and abused to progressive illness and *The Last Girls* explored the dangerous contrast between interior distress and exterior poise, *Guests on Earth* underscores the universality of mental disease. It accomplishes this focus by populating its central setting, Highland Hospital, with mentally ill characters from a variety of walks of life and also by acknowledging the diseased outside the hospital. Evalina's mother Louise, for instance, commits suicide after experiencing severe postpartum depression and the loss of an infant, while Louise's wealthy patrician lover Arthur Graves is later said to have suffered a breakdown and hanged himself.

While these points—that any sort of person can become mentally ill, that the diseased are hospitalized and not—are fairly accessible, Smith presents a more challenging variation of the point in the character of Evalina. The narrator's own take on her sanity is difficult to trust. She inhabits the worlds of the well and the ill and often seems to belong in both, which qualifies her to deliver the novel but also makes it important to question her judgment. Evalina often is perceptive, and much of her wisdom, particularly with regard to romantic relationships, reads as sound. However, she also stops eating for weeks after her mother's death, rendering herself so ill that she is transported to Highland.

Other "breaks" are difficult to classify as depression or reasonable responses to challenging circumstances. Still, the last section of *Guests on Earth* makes it impossible to dismiss these earlier episodes as minor. In that section Evalina initially sounds settled and content: "I am in New Orleans now, where I teach private piano lessons and am proud to be a staff accompanist at the venerable Petit Theatre. I live alone—by choice, I might add—for I have had a few suitors here" (326). She speculates about the fire that destroyed Highland, detailing reasonable explanations for its occurrence.

But then Evalina's writing undergoes an abrupt shift. "I know [Pan] will come to me eventually," Evalina writes, "which is why I settled upon this particular apartment in the Garden district quite near Audubon Park, where he will be able to get a job with the landscaping crew" (327). The idea that Pan, a practically mute forest dweller who casually takes lovers besides Evalina, would follow her across the South to a city apartment is an idea clearly not grounded in reality. Evalina's hopes are more troubling because she does not just daydream about Pan; she plans her activities around the idea that he will arrive. After choosing her underground apartment with Pan in mind, she muses, "I am not yet too old to bear another child." "Pan can learn to speak as the baby speaks, and we will all be very comfortable right here. The apartment is larger than it looks" (328). After a tumultuous early life Evalina cannot entirely distinguish fantasy from reality. She appears to be holding a stable life together, but her ability to sustain that stability for any length of time is questionable.

Considered alongside *Guests on Earth*, *Family Linen,* and *The Last Girls* are notable for the illusion under which their narrators and some characters operate with regard to mental illness. What can seem isolated to both characters and Smith's readers—Fay's inconvenient person, Baby's bouts of illness—clearly never is. *Guests on Earth* takes readers to the hospital they could not enter with Baby, the clinic Fay never saw. Bringing mental illness to the forefront of her novel allows Smith to narrativize the treatment of such diseases and to mine the issues of control inherent in treatment of the mind.

The minds, mostly female, controlled through therapy and shock treatment, medications, and long walks in the woods, are often fiercely intelligent, perceptive, and creative. Dixie, for instance, Evalina's Southern-belle confidant and a former beauty queen, discourses early and often on the difficulty of living as an object of admiration. "Being a belle alone is enough to kill you . . . or ruin you, if you survive," she tells Evalina during their first substantial conversation (145). Dixie's wisdom is hard-won—she combats frequent depression as a mother and wife on her husband's farm—and she often falls silent after periods of intensive treatment by her doctors at Highland. A similar behavior pattern holds on a more dramatic scale in the person of Smith's fictionalized Zelda

Fitzgerald, whose intellect and creativity are staggering. Her advice is much like Dixie's. "'It is far better to be dead than to be a princess in a tower,'" she advises Evalina. "'For you can never get out once they put you up there, you'll see'" (33). Both of these women directly echo Baby Ballou of *The Last Girls,* who expresses her own exasperation with romantic roles. A crucial difference, though, is that Baby does not speak her thoughts in the novel. Instead, Harriet learns of her struggle only by finding and reading Baby's abandoned poems. A particularly apt one reads: "When Jeff first put me up here / I liked it / Oh I liked it a lot / On a clear day / I could see forever. But, though idyllic / this surface is very hard / And the ladder has proved / Retractable / So if you could possibly / Assist me off this pedestal please / It's hurting my ass" (178).

The words of each woman strongly indict romantic love and domestic institutions as factors in mental illness and struggle, and their treatment is guided by similarly male-directed principles. Many characters overtly acknowledge this problem. Dixie, for instance, sees her time at Highland as a fix for her wifely abilities even more than for her happiness. "'I am being reeducated, retrained,'" she tells Evalina. "'For marriage, I guess,' she said. 'I wasn't very good at it before'" (178). Although Dixie sees a return to her home as the aim of her treatment, that space, paradoxically, is the root of damage for her and other women. "'You can give me a truck anytime, over a house,'" another young woman at Highland, Jinx, says in a therapy session. "'Once somebody gets you in a house, they can lock you up in there and do all kinds of things to you, and nobody knows it'" (218). "Home" repeatedly is positioned as a space of entrapment and ill fit for women, rather than a space of creativity, growth, or fulfillment.

Memory

In these three novels treatment of mental illness sometimes involves the reframing of experiences and the understanding of emotions. It often also involves the manipulation of memory. Through shock treatments and hypnosis, especially, characters' recollections are controlled or manipulated, for better and worse, by other characters in positions of authority. Like mental illness, memory is familiar fictional territory for Smith. From Brooke's dissociation with her dead friend Charles in *Something in the Wind* to Molly Petree's desperate attempts to preserve her family's stories in *On Agate Hill,* Smith's characters are inextricable from their recollections of the past.

The manipulation and control of memory are especially dangerous when they are initiated by an outside source. This is not always the case: when Sybill, for instance, unpacks her repressed memories with the help of her hypnotist, she is able to move on from a familial trauma that was causing her physical and emotional damage. Evalina, though, experiences the dangers of memory manipulation. When her physician Dr. Carroll attempts to treat her grief over the suicide of a friend, he decides to administer metrazol convulsion therapy to Evalina. Though other treatments are less risky, Dr. Carroll favors speed over safety in this case, provoking doubts from his wife, a fellow physician, and Evalina herself, who successfully evades the treatment. She later learns that Dr. Carroll believes "women patients in general should be urged to give up their 'unrealistic ambitions' and be 're-educated toward femininity, good mothering, and the revaluing of marriage and domesticity'" (35). While Sybill's hypnotist and most of the Highland doctors seem well meaning, the control they wield over the women they treat is troubling.

As repeat patient at Highland Hospital, Evalina experiences the mixed effects of shock treatments on more than one occasion. Though she feared the manipulation of her memory as a grieving teenager, she embraces it as young woman burdened by two terrible experiences. Shortly after learning that she is the product of incest between her mother and grandfather, Evalina loses her newborn daughter Pietá and finds herself back at Highland with no memory of how she arrived. "Shock treatments do that," she writes. "They rob you of your immediate memory, and in my case, this was a blessing" (131). Evalina's positivity about the treatments is bolstered by her new female psychiatrist, Dr. Schwartz. "Next," Schwartz reassures her, "we may be able to help you form new connections and ways of thinking that are not so painful for you, not overwhelming. So don't worry, you will remember when you are ready to remember" (137). Employed alongside a thoughtful plan rather than as a reckless expedient, memory-altering treatments have appeal for Evalina.

Memory is important for Smith's considerations of severe mental illness and also relevant for characters such as Sybill and Harriet, who are damaged by their pasts in significant, but less dramatic, ways. Smith does not trivialize either of these characters' difficulties, and she is able to treat Sybill's, in particular, with humor. When, for instance, Sybill's physician suggests that her migraine headaches could have a psychological cause, Sybill is reluctant to look for one. At forty-seven years old, she still "regarded her unconscious like she regarded her reproductive system, as a messy, murky, darkness full of unexplained fluids and longings which she preferred not to know too much about" (17). Sybill's discomfort with sexuality and some of her contemporary expressions approximate those of a teenager. "Ugh," she groans when she begins to have "sexy, seedy dreams" alongside her resurfacing memories. She awakens from the dreams and "can't even remember who she is, Ms. Sybill Hess the head of Language Arts at the Roanoke Technical Institute, manager of the Oaks, and not some lowdown hussy" (147). While Sybill is continually prudish and absurd, Smith does not set her up to be a literary punching bag. As she reconciles her returned memories and reconnects with her siblings, Sybill begins to loosen up. She remains tightly wound, but the degree, at least, of her guarded behavior has been a result of her repression.

Hypnosis, the route by which Sybill retrieves her repressed memories, is also mined for humor, but what her sessions uncover is quite serious. Like Evalina, Sybill allows a seemingly well-intentioned man a degree of control over her mind. She follows his commands and is unconscious for hours in his presence. Unlike the imposing Dr. Carroll, though, Bob the hypnotist is a "pudgy little man" whose credentials are unconvincing to Sybill; she calls him "a ridiculous person" (148). Still, Bob's methods are effective. Sybill dreams of her childhood during their second session, and, in the process, begins to remember the night that her father was murdered by a woman she suspects was her mother. Though Sybill's resurfaced memories eventually better her life—in addition to her improved sibling relationships, her headaches end—she initially is furious as she tries to understand what she has witnessed. "She'd rather, on balance, have headaches," she thinks. "The pursuit of truth is worse than headaches in the long run, being more painful" (147).

Unlike Sybill, Harriet is well aware that her memories are the obstacle holding her back from a fulfilling life: she is physically and emotionally handicapped by her surplus of retrievable recollections. In the novel's first few pages Harriet thinks about her lack of energy and lack of a sex life and nearly has a memory-induced panic attack in the lobby of the Peabody Hotel. Many of Harriet's memories are pleasant, but to her they are the wrong memories: "At fifty-three, Harriet can't remember anything, . . . the names of her students . . . [or] the names of her colleagues." In the absence of such practical information she instead "can remember Baby Ballou's beautiful face when she married Charlie Mahan" (3). In addition to feeling the physical effects of her obsession with the past, Harriet is smart enough to see the emotional weight she carries. "Oh, it's too much! Just because Harriet took care of Baby Ballou in college does not mean she has an obligation to do so for the rest of her life" (3). With a tendency toward passivity, Harriet acknowledges her problem with memory but does not act to correct it.

Harriet's immersion in memory is especially intense in the novel's present day, when she accompanies her four college suitemates on a river cruise with the aim of scattering Baby's ashes in the Mississippi. Retracing the voyage that she and her friends made three decades prior increases Harriet's nostalgia, as well as her desire to know if Baby meant to kill herself in her fatal car accident. Though Harriet's interest in the past is often involuntary, she intentionally dwells in memory on the riverboat in hopes of finally deciphering the enigmatic Baby. But clarity continues to elude her. "Who can ever know which story is true? Maybe they're *both* true," she thinks after tossing Baby's ashes into the river. Harriet tries to truly let go of Baby with her toss, even throwing "the box in after her, for good measure," yet Baby is not so easily dismissed. "'Oh my God! She's coming back! Oh no!'" Anna says, as "a little puff of ashes floats back like smoke on the wind" (365). Just as Harriet cannot fully understand Baby, she also cannot entirely be free of her.

At the close of *The Last Girls* Harriet gains a degree of self-absolution by reading a letter from Baby's widower. She "feels an utter fool for torturing herself all these years, for blaming herself, punishing herself for Jeff's death and the wreckage of Baby's life when maybe it wasn't even wrecked. According to Charlie Mahan, it was happy and filled with love" (369). Harriet finally gives herself permission to move on from the losses of her two best friends. "Maybe," the novel's narrator says, "Harriet's own life could have been full and happy, too, if she hadn't felt so guilty" (369). The moment when that thought crosses her mind, when she recognizes not only her guilt but also the degree to which it has controlled her, Harriet experiences a vision in the stars. The "ghost of Baby who sits on a little star swinging her long bare legs" encourages Harriet to move on, and, finally, she does, dancing with the boat's history lecturer, the "Riverlorean" (370). Though Harriet's memories still hold powerful sway over her emotions, the novel's finale suggests that she will find a way to live alongside those memories rather than continuing to bury herself beneath them.

Outside of Evalina, Sybill, and Harriet, who are arguably the main characters in their respective novels, Smith presents other relevant portrayals of characters managing memories. Fay's mental illness in *Family Linen* is, in large part, the result of remembering her traumatic past. In *Guests on Earth* Zelda Fitzgerald vividly remembers summers in Cannes and the sweet face of her daughter Patricia, but she blurs the line between memory and the present by mistaking Evalina for Patricia. Courtney Gray of *The Last Girls* curates her life in scrapbooks, preserving photos in an idealized setting. What Courtney leaves out of her books is as telling as what she includes. "Wouldn't they be amazed," she thinks, "if they knew that the most important person in her life is not even pictured in these albums?" (38). Courtney does not document her affair with the overweight florist Gene Minor or anything else that would sully "the pride of her life" (38). "Gene Minor is just for *her*," she thinks. "He has no business here" (47). Through the successes and failures of these diverse characters, Smith suggests that there are many ways to approach the past, but ignoring it is almost never wise.

While most of the characters in these novels are young-to-middle-aged women, Smith addresses memory in a different population in the short story "The Happy Memories Club," included in both *News of the Spirit* and the

2010 collection *Mrs. Darcy and the Blue-Eyed Stranger.* From the title onward
Smith heavily underscores the importance of memory and the past through
elderly narrator Alice Scully. When Alice's boyfriend begins to forget everything from her name to his internment during the Holocaust, Alice snaps at a
nurse who considers his memory loss "a blessing." "'It is not a blessing, you
ignorant bitch,'" Alice says. "'It is the end. Our memories are all we've got'"
(*Mrs. Darcy* 264). Alice also clashes with her retirement home writing group,
drawing its ire when she shares stories from her life that include suicide, sex,
and other episodes that the group finds scandalous and inappropriate. They
adopt the name the Happy Memories Club in defiance of Alice's full narratives.
Still, Alice is driven to tell her story—"flooded by memories—overwhelmed,
engulfed" as she writes—despite her failing health and the objections of the
writing group (*Mrs. Darcy* 269). Her feisty dedication to remembering is
reminiscent of Ivy Rowe and Molly Petree and of Lee Smith as a woman and
writer. Smith writes in *Dimestore:* "I can't stick to a traditional plot anymore.
I've got plenty of conflict, plenty of complication, but no resolutions in sight.
. . . Life has turned out to be wild and various, full of the unexpected, and it's
a monstrous big river out here" (85).

Friendship

Like much of Smith's fiction, *Family Linen* unspools a family's history, with
particular attention to the damage an older generation inflicts on its descendants. With *The Last Girls* and *Guests on Earth,* though, Smith devotes more
fictional space to friendship. In the latter Smith explores the ways that romantic
love and friendship connect and conflict and the ways that friendships change
over time. In many ways *Guests on Earth* is more concerned with short-term,
transitory friendships. The residents at Highland Hospital frequently move
in and out of one another's lives, appearing and disappearing without explanation. The most interesting perspective on friendship that the novel offers,
though, is its take on the complexities of mentorship. Through Evalina's
interactions with Zelda Fitzgerald and Mrs. Carroll, and even with her one-
time fiancé Freddy, *Guests on Earth* examines the complexities of guidance,
freedom, and artistry.

In *The Last Girls* Harriet's relationship with Baby is complicated by the
girls' shared love of Jefferson Carr. Harriet and Jeff first meet when she is twelve
years old; his father and Harriet's mother have a bittersweet love affair while
Jeff's mother is institutionalized. Described from Harriet's perspective, Jeff is
so wonderful that he is practically magical. When she sees him in college, for
instance, "the clear air went iridescent," and Harriet wonders "how he had simply *appeared*" (151). While Jeff also likes Harriet, he cannot match the strength

of her affection. Instead, he falls instantly for Baby at a party: "Though Jeff kept his hand on her arm and Harriet was still pressed right up against him . . . she knew he had left her. He was there, but somehow he wasn't" (161). Figuratively, Harriet stays in this position for years, rubbing Jeff's shirt between her fingers as he turns his attention to Baby.

Despite his emotional unavailability, Jeff Carr is not abusive in the mold of other brother figures in Smith's fiction. In fact, if not for the resonance of men like *Saving Grace*'s Lamar and Johnny from *The Devil's Dream*, his position as Harriet's near-stepbrother would not be especially troubling. Jeff is not biologically related to Harriet, and he does not often inhabit her house. Significantly, Harriet also is the sexual aggressor in their relationship; Jeff only sleeps with her once, and it is when she climbs into his bed and initiates their encounter. Yet, by casting Jeff as a brother figure to Harriet, Smith cautions readers against overly romanticizing Jeff or his relationship with Harriet. She has taught her audience to be skeptical of brother-sister pairings and thus invites us to question the worth of all Harriet's nostalgia and longing.

While Baby and Jeff are lovers, Harriet's friendship with them is complicated and bittersweet. "From the very beginning, Harriet was a part of it—it was like being in love herself," she thinks, "but not as scary" (163). Jeff and Baby take her on most of their excursions, and she is pleased that "*they* loved her; . . . it was enough. Somehow Harriet was necessary. She completed them" (163). Though Harriet claims to be content with this arrangement, her third-wheel position eventually becomes less fulfilling and unsustainable. At the quarry with Baby and Jeff, for instance, Harriet is conflicted when they disappear into the woods together. "They were crazy," she thinks. "She could not stand to see this, yet she could not stand not to see it either. She hated them both. She hated herself." Alone, Harriet touches herself "until she was gasping in delight or dismay, she couldn't even tell which" (176). What felt like "enough" to Harriet ceases to satisfy her as Jeff and Baby's relationship becomes more physical, and, eventually, more volatile. "'We'll kill each other before we're done,' Baby had said once, but Harriet thought they'd kill *her* first" (177).

Jeff and Baby's difficult breakup brings resentment and anger to the surface in Harriet's friendship with Baby. "You bitch," she says, when Baby admits to breaking up with Jeff. "I can't believe you would do this to him" (296). She takes on the role of the rejected in their conversation, voicing statements and questions from Jeff's perspective. "You think you're so special," Harriet begins. "What is it, you met some other guy, is that it?" (297). When Baby goes to the quarry with a new lover, Harriet feels personally betrayed. "*Where you went with Jeff and me*," she thinks (308). Harriet attempts to preserve her intimate connection to Jeff by blaming Baby and, later, by unsuccessfully pursuing him herself. A single afternoon of desperate, melancholy sex, though, is the last communication Harriet has with Jeff. "She sat by the phone for the next two weeks, willing it to ring, willing it to be for her. But it was always for Baby" (304).

After his afternoon with Harriet, Jeff enlists in the military; he does not answer Harriet's letters, and he is killed in a helicopter accident during training. Harriet withdraws from life, and especially from Baby, for months. When the girls finally cross paths again at Mary Scott College, Harriet is not sure what their friendship looks like. "She couldn't really see Baby at all from this angle," she remarks at one point, suggesting the divide that has grown up between them. Still, Harriet eventually, and somewhat reluctantly, reassures Baby that they are still friends. "'We're okay,' Harriet said, giving Baby everything she wanted, everything she had to have, and oddly enough it *was* okay, though it would never be the same" (316). Though they keep in touch after college, this conversation remains the closest thing to closure that Baby and Harriet achieve in their friendship. It is only after Baby's death that Harriet confronts her memories and progresses in her one-sided resolution.

Although Harriet and Baby's friendship is fundamentally altered in a short period of time *The Last Girls* also depicts the long-term evolution of friendships. When Harriet, Courtney, Anna, and Catherine reunite for their river cruise, they have not seen one another in years. They have become mothers and wives, patients and artists. In some cases their reunion leads to moments of recognition. Harriet, for instance, is initially mystified by Anna's new persona as a famous writer. She spends their first meeting on the riverboat "searching for any trace of the sweet serious friend of her youth" (72). During a late-night conversation, though, the women hint at their experiences with loss. "There's something of Anna here after all," Harriet thinks (81). Harriet's reintroduction to Courtney is less successful. After a few days "Courtney's fed up with Harriet's constant indecision. It's ridiculous, really" (318). Later she regrets that she will leave New Orleans early, "having given up her expensive hotel room to that little twit Harriet" (365). The frostier relationship between one-time friends is partially a product of Courtney's dissatisfaction with her own life but also due to the lack of common interests between Harriet and Courtney. Without their shared experience at Mary Scott College, the women have little to say to one another.

Characters are similarly bound by circumstance at Highland Hospital, where Evalina develops several meaningful friendships that cannot last. Her childhood friend Robert commits suicide after his discharge, while other patients, such as Lily Ponder, simply improve and leave. Thus the sort of closure that Harriet seeks in her relationship with Baby also frequently eludes

Evalina. She sometimes receives news of her friends after they depart, but the chances for goodbyes, and for future correspondence, are limited. "My old chums had dispersed over the summer," Evalina writes of her first friends at the hospital. "It was as if they had all walked into the forest as in 'A Midsummer Night's Dream'" (72). Without long-term peers, Evalina has her most lasting relationships with her caregivers. This situation leads to an imbalance of power in her friendships, whether with her guardian Mrs. Carroll or her doctor Freddy Sledge. Though both attempt to guide her choices, Evalina ultimately distances herself from them, preferring to live without their direct influences.

Mrs. Carroll enters Evalina's life as a mentor figure, teaching her to play the piano and brightening her time at Highland Hospital. "It was my piano lessons that I lived for," Evalina writes, "revering Mrs. Carroll above all others —for her kindness as well as her brilliance" (28). Mrs. Carroll is wealthy, beautiful, talented, and seemingly adored by her husband. Evalina immediately is taken in: "I intended to have a honeymoon in Italy just like Mrs. Carroll. In fact, I intended to be her" (28). As Evalina's own experience and skill grow, however, she begins resent Mrs. Carroll's controlling influence and question the desirability of her life. In addition to buying Evalina's clothing, Mrs. Carroll discourages her friendship with Ella Jean Bascomb, the daughter of a hospital cook. "Ella Jean 'did not come from a nice family,'" Evalina recalls, "by which Mrs. Carroll meant a family in town" (67). When Evalina agrees to study music at the prestigious Peabody School, Mrs. Carroll reveals some of the hidden motivation behind her guidance of Evalina. "'I knew you would not fail me, Evalina,' she said. 'Go, go. Go—you must go, for me. Music is freedom, never forget it'" (101).

From the moment that Evalina recognizes this motivation, her relationship with Mrs. Carroll is cooler and less trusting. "She was *not* free, Mrs. Carroll," Evalina realizes, "her grand career secondary to her famous husband's" (101). The yellow roses gifted weekly to Mrs. Carroll by Dr. Carroll begin to seem less a sign of adoration and more an offering of apology. Yet the distance that arises between mentor and mentee is not solely Evalina's doing. Her postcards to Highland from the Peabody School indicate that Mrs. Carroll, too, feels differently about her mentee. After informing Mrs. Carroll that she plans to train as an accompanist, instead of a solo performer like Mrs. Carroll, Evalina worries that she has upset her teacher. "I wonder if I have done anything to offend you," she writes. "If so, I assure you that it was unintentional" (109). Later postcards reveal that the Carrolls do not attend her concerts and that Mrs. Carroll disapproves of her relationship with the opera singer Joey Nero. Mrs. Carroll genuinely cares for Evalina, but the strings attached to her benevolence complicate their relationship.

Evalina enters her engagement to Freddy Sledge, one of her doctors at Highland, with the lessons she has learned from Mrs. Carroll in mind. Though Freddy is kind and Evalina genuinely likes him, she fears entrapment by marriage. When they kiss, Evalina writes, "I was dismayed to see a clear vision of a princess peering over the battlements of a gingerbread castle" (231). This motif, which Zelda Fitzgerald also invokes as warning, reappears over and over again in *Guests on Earth*. Evalina returns to it when Highland Hospital burns to the ground, killing Zelda and Evalina's friend Dixie, along with seven other women. "The roof began to collapse and they were gone," she recalls, "my princesses, my chums, and it was over. . . . I remembered what Mrs. Fitzgerald had said in Art so long ago, about the danger of putting princesses in towers" (325). With her fear of the castle confirmed, Evalina returns Freddy's engagement ring and leaves Highland to return to New Orleans. There she rents a half-basement, low to the ground and as different from a castle as she can find.

Evalina ostensibly writes all of the material in *Guests on Earth* to share details about Zelda Fitzgerald and the burning of Highland Hospital. "I bring a certain insight," she writes, "and new information to the horrific event that changes all our lives forever" (3). What emerges in her writing, though, is her own narrative, influenced by the likes of Mrs. Carroll, Zelda, and Freddy, but ultimately from her own perspective. Evalina recognizes this as she writes: "This is not my story, then, in the sense that Mr. Fitzgerald's *The Great Gatsby* was not Nick Carraway's story, either—yet Nick Carraway *is* the narrator, is he not? Is any story not always the narrator's story, in the end?" (3). Evalina is only twenty-four years old when the novel concludes, a young woman whose story remains as open-ended as that of any lead character in Smith's fiction.

CHAPTER 7

I Am the One Who Tells the Stories
On Agate Hill

Lee Smith published her twelfth novel, *On Agate Hill*, in the fall of 2006. Though it closely follows 1996s *The Christmas Letters* and 2002s *The Last Girls* in the chronology of Smith's novels, its form and content are more reminiscent of *Oral History* (1983) and *Fair and Tender Ladies* (1988) than they are of those later works. Like *Oral History*, *On Agate Hill* is framed as a historical research project undertaken by a young female student. It does not contain the large number of narrators that *Oral History* does, but its own kind of poly-vocality comes from the various types of fictionalized historical sources that compose it. Diary entries, letters, court documents, and descriptions of found relics are all offered up for examination in the novel. Still, despite this diversity of material, *On Agate Hill* has a focus like that of *Fair and Tender Ladies,* centered as it is on decades in the life of one particular girl, Molly Petree, an orphan whose family breaks apart during and immediately following the U.S. Civil War. It follows Molly as she matures into a young woman, becomes a still-young widow, and reaches old age.

Though elements of *On Agate Hill* are familiar from Smith's earlier novels, its initial Civil War setting is unique in Smith's fiction. Smith had written about undeniably southern locations before, such as when she satirized small-town Alabama in *Fancy Strut*. She had also set plenty of fiction in the past, as she did with the turn-of-the-century mountain setting of *The Devil's Dream*. Until 2006, though, she had not written about the Southern past of plantations, war, and slavery. In an interview with Erica Abrams Locklear, Smith explains her decision to write a more explicitly Southern novel. "I never wrote about or was interested in the Civil War at all," she reveals. "It's just because I had just moved into this house . . . right next door to the Civil War cemetery, and it has this legend associated with it . . . I just got interested" (227–28). Inspired by her house's past, Smith began the historical research that would become *On Agate Hill*, working at both the nearby Orange County Historical Museum and the Burwell School Historic Site. In her acknowledgments she also writes of visiting Stagville Plantation and Bennett Place, and of reading diaries, oral histories, and memoirs to inform her novel. Growing as it did from Smith's Hillsborough home, *On Agate Hill* is, as Smith told Martha Waggoner of the *Milwaukee Journal,* "such a private book and such a very local book."

Smith calls the book "private" because, although the novel's beginning arose from her move to Hillsborough, she continued to write it largely because of her son Joshua Seay, who died suddenly in 2003 at the age of thirty-three. She initially abandoned the novel after his death. But when a therapist suggested she "get out of [her] own head for a while every day," Smith resumed working. "It's Josh's book," she has said, and "it's a piece of my heart" (Waggoner). In addition to dedicating the book to her son, Smith included Josh by inscribing him into the narrative; the character Juney, whom Lucinda MacKethan calls "a wise and winsome listener," ("Multiple Personality Disorder") is based on Josh. As Smith tells it: "Through the mysterious alchemy of fiction, my sweet Josh had managed to find his own way into the final pages of the novel after all, as a mystical bluesman and healer living wild and free at last in the deep piney woods he used to play in as a child" (Smith "Showing Up for Work"). Though *On Agate Hill* is less obviously autobiographical than some of Smith's work, it is infused with her experience of loss.

On Agate Hill is most distinguished in Smith's fiction by its unique setting, but it also is structurally innovative. Smith's use of a variety of fictionalized sources, which reflect those she consulted in writing the novel, underscores her continued emphasis on telling alternate versions of history by calling attention to the oral or otherwise unconventional narratives of persons not often represented in history textbooks. That these intratextual artifacts—diaries, court testimony, and letters, particularly—are either meant to be private or to represent an individual's subjective view also suggests Smith's belief that the past is open to subjective interpretation, even by those who lived it. The most striking of these stories is that of Simon Black, a former Confederate soldier who makes his postwar fortune in Brazil. Smith upends stereotypes of the Southern gentleman through Black's story and undermines romantic notions of plantation life through Molly's. On Agate Hill, former slaves are kind but not blindly loyal, and they are in relatively intimate contact with their former masters.

Molly's story, particularly, is suggestive of ideas about family, memory, and loss. With most of her biological family dead before she reaches age thirteen,

Molly tries to balance her perceived responsibility to remember these people and their stories with her desire to form new connections. By positioning herself as a "ghost girl," Molly anchors herself in her family's past—some of which she was not alive for—even as she exists in its present. Minrose Gwin has written about situations such as Molly's in the history of the South: "Cultural memory and mourning kept alive through writing and stories are as much spatial as temporal," she observes. They "exist in both the past and the present, yet they move us toward a future that will inevitably become the past" (From the Gwin work "Introduction: Reading History, Memory, and Forgetting" 1). Molly's memories are both derived from Agate Hill and of greater importance to her when she lives there. Though her memories burden Molly sometimes, they sustain her in others. She derives particular sustenance from them in the last section of the novel, when she returns to the old plantation. Molly modifies her idea about what constitutes a family when she returns.

Like Ivy Rowe before her, Molly Petree gains a sense of herself by writing, a pursuit in which she engages for decades of her life. She also shares Ivy's tendency to create "doubles" for herself and mirrors Ivy's desire for a community of women from whom she can draw strength. Unlike Ivy's voice, however, Molly's is informed by her formal education. As a student and, eventually, a teacher, Molly uses her diary and her lessons to establish her identity and sort through the events of her life. The most significant impact of Molly's education may be that she leaves her diary intact to be unearthed by Tuscany Miller. While Ivy burns her letters, citing the importance of process over product, Molly preserves a record of her life, an action which is consistent with her desire to keep her family's stories and memories alive.

Smith's belief that her novel was personal made its largely favorable critical reviews surprising to her. One particularly positive review came from Donna Rifkind of the *Washington Post,* who wrote that despite *On Agate Hill*'s tricky subject matter, Smith "never allows her narrative to slip into kitsch, stereotype, or melodrama." The *Atlanta Journal Constitution* reviewer Diane Roberts was equally impressed by Smith's "command of her talent for strong stories and evocative characters," calling the novel her "best yet." Still, not all critics were as enthusiastic. The *New York Times*'s Roy Hoffman, for instance, was measured in his acclaim for the novel, praising Smith's ability to "[bring] to life children who see much and tell all," but alleging that Molly's childhood writing was "too good to be true . . . too conspicuously guided by the hand of the author."

Roberts and other reviewers, effusive or reserved, often compared *On Agate Hill* both to Smith's earlier novels and to the works of other writers. Hoffman, for example, likens Molly Petree to the heroines of Frances Hodgson Burnett's novels *The Secret Garden* and *The Little Princess,* characterizing all three as "smart, dreamy girls, wrenched from happy childhoods by the loss of their parents." Donald Harington of the *Raleigh News and Observer* used chronology as a basis to draw comparisons with other novels published in the fall of 2006, asserting that *"On Agate Hill* will not merely hold its own with the best of them, but also will serve as a model for future writers of historical fiction." That Smith's novel was published alongside works by Thomas Pynchon and Charles Frazier, who also set their 2006 novels *Against the Day* and *Thirteen Moons,* respectively, in the nineteenth century, makes this praise even more striking.

Smith's historical novel also naturally invites comparisons to fiction about the Civil War period in U.S. history. The most obvious of these is to Margaret Mitchell's hugely popular *Gone with the Wind* (1936), which also features a plantation setting and includes scenes that occur after the war's end. While Mitchell's novel examines "genteel poverty" and emphasizes its heroine's pursuit of material wealth, however, *Agate Hill* approaches postbellum plantation life from a more somber perspective. One example of this difference is that the slaves of Tara supposedly are glad to stay and serve Scarlett after the war, but Molly's family's former slaves depart in the night, unwilling to stay as Agate Hill deteriorates; another is that Molly never materially rebuilds Agate Hill but instead reconstructs something resembling a family life within its crumbling walls.

The novel also resonates with another work from Mitchell's era, William Faulkner's 1938 novel *The Unvanquished.* As in *On Agate Hill,* Faulkner's novel employs a then-young narrator to describe the war's domestic aftermath. The teenager Bayard Sartoris is good friends with Ringo, a young former slave living on his family's plantation, much as Molly is with Washington. In both novels these friendships lead to the blurring of racial boundaries that unsettles older relatives of the white characters. In *On Agate Hill* Molly's familiarity with Washington upsets her prim Aunt Cecilia, while in *The Unvanquished* Bayard and his grandmother move into one of the slave cabins after Union soldiers torch their house. Smith evokes *The Sound and the Fury* here, too, when Molly attempts to bury Simon Black at a farm relatively near Agate Hill. "No one had told me that it had become a golf club," Molly writes, "dotted with golfers and caddies" (349). The transformation from ancestral family land to sport club recalls the appropriation of the Compson land in the 1929 novel.

As she did with *Fair and Tender Ladies,* Barbara Bates Smith adapted *On Agate Hill* for the stage, playing each of the novel's primary characters in her one-woman show. Jim Cavener of the *Asheville Citizen-Times* reviewed a performance of the play at the North Carolina Stage Company, calling Bates Smith "a marvel as she slipped from character to character." Bates Smith signaled her move from one character to the next by placing a "signature item" representative of each character on a table, and by modifying her voice to channel each. Cavener also praised the "talented vocal, banjo, and hammer dulcimer score by Jeff Sebens," who used songs "both familiar and new" to accompany Bates Smith's performance. The play's musical component reflects the importance of music in the novel itself; Molly's wild husband Jacky Jarvis comes from a family of talented musicians, and the "evidence" in Tuscany's box includes a ballad, "Molly and the Traveling Man" (308). As in *The Devil's Dream,* music is a family affair in *On Agate Hill.*

In 2012 Bates Smith used pieces of her Agate Hill show for a new production, *Agate Hill to Appomattox: Southern Women's Voices.* The play, which draws from *On Agate Hill,* Allan Gurganous's *Oldest Living Confederate Widow Tells All,* and Ron Rash's story collection *Burning Bright,* premiered in Chapel Hill, North Carolina, on June 8, 2012. The Agate Hill portion of the production centers on Molly's return to Agate Hill and the childhood memories that her return evokes. By juxtaposing Smith's novel with other recent Civil War fictions, Bates Smith showcases the prominent role that female characters have played in these publications.

Alternate Histories

In *On Agate Hill* Smith continues to invite her readership to consider histories that fall outside dominant historical narratives. By setting a Civil War novel after the conflict's end, Smith is able to fictionalize material and psychological effects of the war that would not be fully apparent when battles still were waged. She writes, for instance, of how racial dynamics between former slaves, still living on plantations, and their onetime owners change after the conflict and of whether traumatized soldiers are reintegrated, or not, into postbellum society. Smith's focus on the home front does not mean, however, that the novel is concerned only with the war's legacy for women and children or other domestic figures. While Smith does focus a great deal of attention on characters who never see battle—Molly Petree, Selena Vogell, and Junius Hall, especially—one of the most striking stories she includes is that of Simon Black, a Confederate soldier who fled the United States after watching his army's surrender at Bennett farmhouse. Through Black's narrative, which is revealed in a letter he writes to Molly Petree, Smith plumbs the relatively obscure history of *Confederados,* mostly male white Southerners who emigrated to South America after the Civil War. She also continues her practices of showcasing nontraditional sources of historical information and of subverting stereotypes about historical figures. Though Simon Black is a wealthy former soldier born on a plantation, his wealth is self-made, he fled war, and his plantation residence was in an outbuilding with his blacksmith father. Including this historical perspective is one way that Smith, intentionally or not, participates in what Susan V. Donaldson has called "the necessity of responding to and writing against the long shadow cast by *Gone with the Wind* on popular memories of slavery, the antebellum South, and the Civil War era" (268). (Donaldson cites works by Toni Morrison, Edward P. Jones, and Valerie Martin as especially concerned with altering popular perceptions of the era with respect to slavery.)

In *On Agate Hill* Smith has created what critic David W. Price calls a "poietic history," one that "present[s] us with the emotional, psychological, and intellectual dimensions [of history] that we experience from the inside of a fictional character or imagined situation" (2). The novel's historical story is framed by the twenty-first-century narration of Tuscany Miller, a young woman seeking readmission to a "documentary studies program" (1). After Tuscany's father and his partner move into a "completely run down plantation," they give Tuscany a box filled with historical relics; she forwards it to a former professor in hopes of reentering his program. Though Tuscany has a gratingly modern voice—her commentary on the teacher Mariah Snow's diary, for instance, is "She was so weird" (127)—her inclusion in the novel serves two significant functions. First, Tuscany is a plausible source for the historical items that she sends her professor. Because the items are so varied in their origins and authorship, it makes good narrative sense to explain how, through Tuscany, they came to be grouped together. More important, though, Tuscany acts as a humorous surrogate for Smith herself. The process by which Tuscany gathers historical documents and pieces them together to shape the history of Molly Petree is not unlike the process by which Smith researched *On Agate Hill*. Both Smith and her narrator were introduced to their material by a move to a historic house, and, though she likely gives herself too little credit, Smith claims to have felt that she, like Tuscany, did little more than editorial work in writing the novel. In her words, "it just took off and wrote itself" ("Showing Up for Work"). That an investigator as seemingly hapless as Tuscany can unearth and become immersed in such a rich history suggests the power of the relics, themselves—diaries and letters and court documents offer a more intimate look at the past than would the average history textbook.

The novel's first historical document, Molly Petree's diary, tells of life at Agate Hill plantation in 1872 and 1873, approximately seven years after the Confederate army's surrender. Most of Molly's immediate family has died, and the thirteen-year-old diarist lives with her despondent Uncle Junius, his servant and eventual wife Selena Vogell and her children, and a few of the family's former slaves. Through Molly's precocious voice, Smith fictionalizes the war's psychological aftermath for a damaged soldier and the way it initially altered social and racial relations on a former plantation. The soldier in question is Spencer Hall, Molly's cousin. Spence, as he is called, "walked home from the war Insane" and lives in nearby house with Romulus, "a skinny mean looking negro man with scars on his cheeks [who] used to be the slave driver" (104).

Romulus's name carries associations with memory that, while nonexistent in 1872, suggest his role as a sort of sacrificial reservoir for Spence. He is nick-named Rom, which is homographic with ROM, the commonly used acronym for a specific type of computer memory. ROM is where information that starts the computer is stored, and its makeup cannot be changed without a great deal of effort. Thus Rom potentially is associated, for twenty-first-century readers, with ingrained memories, which he carries along with his physical scars. Like Ivy and Silvaney of *Fair and Tender Ladies*—one wild but insane, the other able to cope—Rom and Spence are two halves of an unusual whole: while Spence seems to remember nothing of the war, Rom bears the burden of memory.

The physical proximity in which these men, one white, one black, live together is accepted as a matter of course at Agate Hill. But when Molly's stern Aunt Cecilia visits, the socially transgressive nature of this arrangement is highlighted. After a group of "ruffians" from town comes looking for Romulus, Cecilia scolds Junius for encouraging Romulus's "manner" and says that "it is just not right for Spencer to live out there" (61). Cecilia's words are not enough to bring about a change in Spence and Rom's relationship, but the two are eventually violently separated by their community. After a group of men attack Rom for speaking to a white woman behind the counter of a store, Spence enters the fight and is shot in the head. Spence's death reiterates the precarious nature of his arrangement with Rom.

By bringing an outsider, Cecilia, into the isolated world of Agate Hill, Smith catalyzes Molly's recognition of the many ways in which Uncle Junius rejects societal norms pertaining to race and class. Cecilia is aghast, for instance, that Molly spends much of her time playing with Washington, the son of a slave and Molly's "best friend on this place" (9). Her outrage intensifies when she realizes that Washington has been taught to read, an action she considers "'the very height of irresponsibility'" (63). Still, Cecilia stays on at Junius's planta-tion despite her objections to the racial dynamic there because she believes she can change it; she busies Washington with chores that keep him from Molly's company. What Cecilia cannot abide, though, are the lapses in class distinction that Junius allows after the passing of his wife, Fannie. Specifically, Cecilia vehemently protests Junius's sexual relationship with Selena, the wife of his former tenant farmer, whom Cecilia calls his "gypsy whore" in front of Molly (62). When she realizes that Junius intends to marry Selena—thus making her heiress to what remains of Agate Hill—Cecilia leaves the plantation rather than remain to see it happen. By highlighting Cecilia's opposition to the union of Junius and Cecilia, Smith draws a provocative parallel between treatment of race and class. Cecilia's words and actions recall the tradition of the white southern male bound to protect white southern womanhood from the threat of miscegenation. As with other tropes in the novel, though, Smith turns this one around; in *On Agate Hill* it is the defiantly aristocratic southern woman determined to prevent her low-class counterpart from accessing the bed—and, not insignificantly, the inheritance—of the poor helpless southern male.

If Smith begins to subvert the type of the southern gentleman in the tale of Uncle Junius, Selena, and Cecilia, she continues to do so even more provocatively with the story of Simon Black, a tale revealed late in the novel. Black is a representative of Confederate Civil War veterans in the novel. This figure, as Caroline Gebhard has written, "was ubiquitous in American fiction after the Civil War; in his ramrod posture, his integrity verging on absurdity, and above all in his unfailing sense of his own dignity, he embodied (white) southern male honor and pride" (133). Representations of this type—"Colonels," Gebhard calls them—are often are invested with "glamour and pathos, especially dramatized through their sentimental relations with their manservants." Smith's version of this character, Simon Black, is Molly's mysterious benefactor and admirer of her mother, Alice. Before he confides in Molly via a letter, Black seems much like one of Gebhard's Colonels. A wealthy former Confederate soldier, he is endlessly dedicated to Molly because of a promise he made to her mother, the object of his unrequited love. The personal and financial interest he takes in her do, unexplained, seem absurd; Black also travels with a mysterious manservant, Henry, at his beck and call. As a young woman, Molly resents his presence in her life, annoyed at intercessions and advice that she has not requested and does not understand.

By imbuing Black with many of these qualities, Smith creates a parallel between her postbellum man of mystery and these popular Confederate veteran types. However, once she suggests their resemblance, Smith subverts the type by adding unexpected depth and vision to the character of Simon Black. In his letter to Molly, which she reads after his death, Black reveals a personal history that is both surprising and educational. For instance, while Black has the great financial resources of a stereotypical Southern gentleman, he is revealed to have amassed them in South America, where he fled, devastated, after deserting the Confederate army. As his letter continues, his position as a familiar figure further erodes: his plantation upbringing was as a lowly blacksmith's son, and Henry, never his slave, instead traveled with him from Brazil. The myth of the postbellum Southern gentleman, campy or not, does not always hold up under close examination. Simon Black initially fits the fictional type, but once his character is known, he turns the trope on its head. Simon Black's narrative gives Smith an opportunity to present the history of *Confederados*, Southerners who emigrated to South America during and after the conflict.

Smith also highlights postbellum rural education in *On Agate Hill*. Although the novel's plantation setting is the most resonant setting in the novel—Molly's return to it, as an aged woman, brings her story full circle and to its close—Smith also unearths a relatively unexplored history in the mountains of North Carolina, where Molly and her teacher and friend Agnes Rutherford begin their own school. The mountain setting provides an opportunity for Smith to explore nineteenth-century rural education and the so-called Moonlight Schools, where adults could attend evening classes. "It was surprising how many [students] there were," Agnes writes, "and how badly they wanted to learn, walking the long roads home at all hours, often sleeping on the schoolhouse floor" (240). As Smith highlights this unconventional education, she also gives her reading audience an informal introduction to the history of these schools. Similarly, Smith's readers share in the rudimentary history lessons that Molly and Agnes receive upon their arrival in the mountains. "We were once part of the State of Franklin," fellow teacher Felix Boykin tells them, "an area formed from western North Carolina and eastern Tennessee which seceded from the Union right after the Revolutionary War" (226). Smith reveals here that, like the southern states, Appalachia historically has been separated at times from the northern United States; she also underscores the separation that exists between Appalachia and the rest of the South of which it geographically is a part. By moving the plot of her most Southern—with a capital S—novel to a rural mountain community not unlike those in some of her earlier novels, Smith gestures toward a connection between Appalachian and Southern histories.

Memory and Family

Molly Petree's early diary entries feature a sad refrain. "I am an orphan girl," she writes on its very first page; "I live in a house of ghosts" (7). Molly is physically without most of her family, but her frequent references to ghosts suggest the powerful degree to which they remain with her through stories, memories, and the artifacts of Agate Hill. Molly echoes and expands upon her relationship with these ghosts as she writes, saying, for instance, "I can not go. For I am the only one left in the world who remembers these ghosts, who thinks of them now, and if I go then they will be gone too" (20). Molly feels a responsibility to record and steward her family's past, an obligation that stems both from her loneliness without them and from her desire to memorialize them. Molly's desire, according to David Lowenthal, is a fictional element that is common in the real world. "In recoiling from grievous loss or fending off a fearsome future," he has written in one study of how people grapple with the past, "people the world over revert to ancestral legacies" ("Possessed" xiii). That Molly's ghosts continue to resurface when she is no longer an imaginative child and when she does not reside at Agate Hill suggests their enduring influence on her life. As Minrose Gwin has written, "the 'ghosts' in the stories of southern history uncannily appear time and time again . . . [in] the mourning for family and community" ("Introduction" 6). Molly's ghosts literally appear within the space of the novel, but haunting also occurs outside the novel as a result of *On Agate Hill*. By offering Molly's fictional story to her reading audience, Smith raises old southern ghosts in the contemporary world.

Molly has appropriated stories about her family from before she was alive and from when she was very young as her own memories, retelling them in her diary as though she lived them herself. "It was a summer evening and the house at Agate Hill was jam packed full of visitors as always," Molly begins one tale. "Little children [were] already asleep on a pallet upstairs while the others were finishing supper *such as it was*, Mamma always said when she told this story" (23). By incorporating her mother's phrases into her own writing, Molly both reveals the frequency with which her mother told her the story and attempts to preserve something of Alice; remembering the story itself is important but so is remembering the language in which it was told. Molly also participates in the creation of a small-scale collective memory by dwelling in (hi)stories that are not her own. It is apparent that Molly's family's past is, at least initially, the primary way that Molly forms her identity because of the notable frequency with which she calls herself a "ghost" girl. Although Molly's tendency to conflate her remembered experiences with stories told by her mother and other family members seems exceptional, Jacques Le Goff notes that it is relatively common for children to assume the memories of others. "The history of our childhood," he writes, "is composed not only of our own first memories, but also of our parents' memories, and this part of our temporal perspective develops on the basis of both these components" (3). Thus, though Molly is a small child during the Civil War, her "temporal perspective" allows her to memorialize the conflict in her writing and her mind.

Though she writes pages about her own family's past, Molly also is a sometimes reluctant repository for impressions of the past not directly gleaned from her family. She provides accounts that balance or contradict the Petree-Hall historical perspective even as she faithfully records that perspective. When, for instance, she and Mary White see "a negro hanging by the neck from a rope attached to a big old oak tree," Molly feels compelled to spread the word about the body and to record the incident in her diary. She also tells Mary White the other stories she has heard about violence against black persons, despite Mary White's reluctance to hear. "I don't know why I always have to know things like that," she writes, "why I have to go on like that, but I do. It is the way I am. I always have to know everything" (80). Although Molly's familial experience of slavery has been with the institution in a comparatively gentle guise, she does not turn away from harsher histories that coexist with her family's stories and experience; instead she actively seeks information about the larger world.

By providing context for her family's perspective, Molly both grounds their stories and underscores their exceptionalism. Her actions evoke another argument by Lowenthal, who writes that "no physical object . . . is an autonomous guide to bygone times; they light up the past only when we already know they belong to it" (*The Past* 238). Molly's writing "lights up the past" of the objects that she and Mary White collect and examine. When, for instance, she and Mary White find a hand bone, which they call the Yankee Hand, they save the item and write about it, too. "We wrapped the bones in honeysuckle," Molly writes; "now [they] are here in a fancy little box I have had forever, just waiting" (53). Molly and Mary White eventually have an entire collection of "phenomena," but, unlike most of Molly's stories, the histories the girls create about the objects in their collection are not especially true. There is no evidence that the Yankee Hand is actually from a deceased Union soldier; rather, Molly and Mary White invent the hand's origin story based upon the spot where they find it. Molly's imagination and awareness of historical events outside of her family's past make her an ideal historical narrator for Smith: she assembles concrete artifacts, imaginative memories, newspaper accounts, and oracular stories to shape her own historical perception.

The urgency of Molly's need to remember is underscored by her juxtaposition with Spence, Junius's son who seems to remember nothing about his life after he returns from the Civil War. When she sees Spence, Molly writes, "I think, which is worse? To remember nothing or to remember too much, like me?" (104). Although Molly does not put her affliction in any sort of clinical terms, her complaint resembles hypermnesia, which Michael Roth calls "the disease of too much memory" (5). Though Molly is generally able to function under the weight of the past, her determination to remember aligns with some of Roth's criteria for sufferers of hypernesia; Molly's memory can be "an agent of disorder, overwhelming the present" and "throwing [other features of her life] out of balance" (16). When, for instance, Molly is unable to accompany Nora Gwyn, the wife of a local preacher, to attend school in Tennessee, Molly hides from Nora and cries alone. "I am a big girl and too old to cry," she explains, "but I know I will never see her again. Every time somebody leaves here, we never see them again" (23). Molly's past losses have left her fearful of the present, and they also lead to conflicts with the people with whom she must live instead of her family.

Though Molly often writes of her need to remember as though it is a burden or even a disease, like Ivy Rowe of *Fair and Tender Ladies* she also emotionally depends upon her family's memories and stories. While she cries about Nora Gwyn's departure, for instance, she distracts herself by listing the living and dead inhabitants of Agate Hill and recalling a few of Alice Petree's stories. Her dependence is most striking, though, when she is harassed by Nicky Eck, a visiting friend of Selena's who is a "smooth-talking smooth-haired traveling man" (115). Nicky molests and eventually rapes Molly; in her efforts to avoid him she retreats to her cubbyhole to create imaginative renderings of her family, who, she writes, "are stuck in time as I am stuck in here" (118). The vignettes she records in isolation, short glimpses of her mother, father, and younger brother Willie, are not particularly cheerful—her father's includes the line "he will be blown to smithereens by a bursting shell then gathered up in pieces and buried beneath a green willow tree"—but they do temporarily distract her from Nicky Eck's advances. However, when she finally leaves the cubbyhole only to be raped by Nicky, the horror of her present is strong enough to undo the somber magic of her memories. "I will be going away now Dear Diary," Molly writes; "I do not care that I am leaving my ghosts" (122). Molly does leave Agate Hill for Gatewood Academy and eventually the Bobcat School after her rape, but her ghosts do not disappear.

Molly's vacillating reliance upon and rejection of memories is deeply tied to her complex feelings about family; her emotional reliance on her memories persists, with a few interruptions, largely because they are the only access she has to most of her biological family. That Molly uses even dark stories from her parents' pasts to distract herself suggests the comfort that she takes in the mere idea of having a family. She would rather think of her father "blown to smithereens" than not think of him at all. Still, as Molly ages and grows, there are times when she distances herself from her ghosts. When she leaves Agate Hill for Gatewood Academy, for instance, Molly immerses herself in the social life of boarding school, spending holidays with the family of her friend Eliza and receiving "gentleman caller[s]" (193). However, despite her efforts to dismiss her ghosts, they return, unbidden, in disruptive ways. Selena's son Godfrey finds her at school to tell her about Spence's death, and the news sends Molly into a near-catatonic state. As her friend and teacher Agnes writes, "the incident has brought back sad memories from her childhood which might have best been forgotten" (178). Molly is thrust back into the past by the news of Spence, and she writes to Mary White about "giving up and going to join [her] ghost family" (182). The extreme reaction that Molly has to Spence's death suggests that, despite external signs that she has left her family's past behind at Agate Hill, Molly is still one letter or visit away from being overtaken by it again.

She is visited by the ghosts of the past again at her Gatewood Academy graduation ceremony, where Molly is surrounded by the families of her classmates. "No one had come to commencement for me, no one was missing me now," she writes to Mary White. "No matter how much I have tried to fool myself, in that instant I knew the truth. I am still an orphan girl, loose in the world, and do you know what, Mary White? I *like* it that way!" (198). After her paralysis at the news of Spence's death, Molly is better able to handle visitations from her ghosts; she is still devastated by the absence of her family, but she identifies herself with them rather than trying to distance herself from them.

It is when Molly marries Jacky Jarvis and begins a new family in North Carolina that her relationship to her memories and ghosts truly changes. Consumed by her passionate love for Jacky and devastated by the loss of her babies, Molly seems to live in the present rather than the past. The word *seems* is appropriate here because *On Agate Hill* never provides a firsthand contemporaneous account of Molly and Jacky's marriage; impressions and stories from that time are instead glimpsed through court testimony, letters and diary entries Molly drafted after Jacky's death, and the lyrics of a song. Still, Smith hints that Jacky will enable Molly to move on from her family's history as soon as the two meet. Molly immediately tells Jacky all about her past, revealing details to him that previously had lived only in her diary and letters. Molly's talking suggests the strength of her connection to Jacky, and its literary precedent in Smith's novels also implies that Molly will achieve some degree of healing through it. When Smith's characters, such as Sally of *Oral History* and Ivy Rowe of *Fair and Tender Ladies* find a person to whom they can, and do, speak freely, they flourish and grow. While Molly has Jacky, she is too busy and engaged to be ruled by her ghosts. When she loses him, though, and is tried for his murder, Molly would rather return to her old ghosts than live in her marital home without Jacky. "I can't live here anymore, not after all that has happened," she tells BJ, Jacky's cousin who was his actual killer (325). Molly's reaction contrasts starkly with her earlier duty to safeguard family memories at Agate Hill, a difference that she poetically explains: "I remembered how, as a girl, I thought I could not leave Agate Hill, that I could not leave my ghosts. Now I understood that love does not reside in places, neither in the Capulets' tomb nor the dales of Arcady nor the Kingdom by the Sea nor in any of those poems that Mary White and I read so long ago, love lives not in places nor even bodies but in the spaces between them, the long and lovely sweep of air and sky, and in the living heart and memory until that is gone too, and we are all of us wanderers, as we have always been, upon the earth. I was free to go" (328). Molly returns to her memories after Jacky's death, but this time her husband is one of the ghosts whom she recalls. In prison Molly recollects, "I was too busy remembering Jacky, memorizing him, every inch of his body, every expression on his face" (313).

Molly has cause to mourn and memorize Jacky, as he is the great love of her life. Their marriage suggests what Ivy Rowe might have had, had she been able to keep Honey Breeding. Linda Byrd Cook argues that "Jacky, like Honey, is a 'back door man' . . . a wanderer, a free spirit" (208). Jacky is a musician, and he gives Molly a community by taking her to live near his extended family in the mountain hamlet of Plain View. Though their passion is never in doubt, Molly does not change Jacky's restless spirit. Wrecked by the death of their two-year-old daughter Christabel and a heartbreaking number of stillbirths, he begins multiple affairs, at least one of which results in a handful of illegitimate children with a woman named Icy Hinshaw. Molly's response to Jacky's infidelities suggests the depths of her love for him. After Jacky has died, Molly goes to see his children and then asks BJ to give Icy and her children the home where she and Jacky lived. "Give them this house and take care of them," she says, "for they are Jacky's. They are yours" (325). Theirs has not been an easy or conventional marriage, but on her deathbed Molly does not regret it. "I am glad I gave all my heart," she writes; "I would do it again" (359).

When Molly, now in her forties, returns to Agate Hill to find Simon Black on his deathbed, she reaches a relative peace with the ghosts of her past, a group which now includes Jacky and Christabel. Molly grapples with her memories and her identity in the old house, a process catalyzed by learning new information about her family's past even as she mourns her most recent losses. Simon Black's letter, for instance, which Molly reads after his death, explains his relationship with Alice and helps Molly to feel a connection with her long-dead mother. What really enables Molly to coexist more ably with her ghosts, though, is her embrace of the living alongside the dead. Rejecting the isolation that she sought at Agate Hill as a girl, Molly waits twenty years to enter her cubbyhole, busying herself instead with Simon, Henry, and Juney. Rather than repeatedly terming herself a "ghost" or a steward of memories, Molly bestows more active, literal titles upon herself. "I am the one who adds up the sums and tells the stories," she writes in her diary; "Henry is the one who drives the car" (354). Molly certainly does not forget her ghosts, but she is more willing to feel love and purpose in the world of the living; she accepts Henry and Juney, especially, as family. She manages, in her final years, to create a fulfilling life by cobbling together an unconventional sort of family in the crumbling remains of Agate Hill.

Identity and Education

Because *On Agate Hill* follows Molly Petree from her adolescence until she is old, it chronicles circumstances and events that cause shifts in her identity. Though these shifts often are catalyzed by changes in Molly's physical, geographical location, they also occur in response to loves, losses, and formal education. Molly ends her diary at the same place, Agate Hill, where she began it, and the circularity of her physical journey mirrors that of her identity over time; at the end of her life Molly feels like she has returned to the self of her girlhood. Smith shows us about Molly's subjectivity mostly through the character's own writing, but other voices, such as those of teachers and friends, occasionally provide glimpses of Molly from different perspectives. Still, Molly's self-reflexive writing provides a compelling portrait of her conception of her own identity, which she largely reveals by drawing comparisons between herself and others, women especially, whom she encounters. Molly initially resists being likened to her mother Alice, even as she relishes her bond with her cousin Mary White and her teacher-turned-colleague and friend Agnes Rutherford. Because Molly inhabits spaces both Southern and Appalachian, her subjectivity suggests similarities and differences between those regions of the country.

In the earliest pages of her diary Molly defines herself by her family and her isolation. "I am like a ghost girl wafting through this ghost house seen by none," Molly writes, tying herself to her dead relatives rather than to living persons. From her cubbyhole in the plantation she listens to noises in the house and watches the activity outside. "I can see everything. . . . Everything! But nobody can see me" (19). Molly's isolation is appealing to her because of her dislike of some other residents of Agate Hill, but it also allows her to indulge her curiosity about everything and everyone, a trait she recognizes. "I mean to write in secrecy and stealth the truth as I see it," she writes; "I will write it all down every true thing in black and white upon the page, for evil or good it is my own true life and I WILL have it" (7–8). Molly's early emphasis on truth and knowing implies that, though she is only thirteen years old, she already is disillusioned with a perceived lack of truth or insight in the world. Her defiant claims to her life, too, suggest a precocious dedication to her subjectivity, fluid as it may be. That Molly variously refers to herself, in the space of just one page, as "an orphan girl," "a spitfire and a burden," a "refugee girl," and a "ruby-throated hummingbird" suggests that Molly is trying on identities and self-concepts as she writes, aided by her vivid imagination in her search for self-definition (7). What her metaphors suggest she has figured out is that she is isolated and unsettled, still ungrounded after an early life "dragged from pillar to post" (7).

The role into which Molly most frequently casts herself is guardian of her family's past. One important consequence of this role for Molly's identity, though, is the comparisons it causes her to draw between herself—and the deceased family members with whom she aligns herself—and the people who replace her family at Agate Hill, primarily Selena, who steadily assumes control of the plantation in the absence of such women as Alice Petree and Fannie Hall. Even before Aunt Cecilia arrives to highlight Selena's transgression of social norms, Molly expresses her resentment of the housekeeper-turned-lady-of-the-house. "Selena has got notions," Molly writes; "in fact she is full to bursting with them" (27). Using the language of the privileged, Molly accuses Selena of trying to "worm her way into this house" and describes her hold on Junius as "like poison ivy" (28). Molly's language is more emotionally charged when she sees Selena wearing Alice Petree's jewelry. "It kills me to see Mammas jade ring from the Orient on the little finger of Selenas fat hand," she writes, "and the coral bead necklace around her neck, I wish it would choke her dead" (13). Molly resents Selena's attempts to fill the places of Fannie Hall and Alice Petree, but it is not clear, despite her strong language, that she feels this way because of Selena's social status. In fact, Molly frequently expresses her admiration of Selena's strength and work ethic, and she herself prefers outdoor labor to relaxing indoors as her mother once did. Molly writes that Selena is "a tall woman strong as an ox" who "can work all day long in the field then split wood like a man" (28). This description is as close to praising Selena as she can come, though, until she is much older. When Molly returns to Agate Hill and discovers the buried bones of Selena's husband Mr. Vogell, she understands that Selena killed him and finds a point of identification in that desperate act. "Perhaps this is why I hated her so much," Molly muses, "because I knew— even then—that I was exactly like her, skin and bone, tooth and claw. I would have done anything at all to have my Jacky" (350). Though we may disagree with Molly's self-characterization, her admission of likeness with Selena suggests the perspective she has gained by living away from Agate Hill.

Despite her initial rejection of Selena in favor of Fannie and her mother Alice, Molly is also disinclined to identify with those women in her early diary entries. She writes of Fannie with warmth and love but resents her dedication to motherhood, which ultimately caused her death. "I will NEVER have a baby myself," Molly writes, recalling the delivery of her dead cousin Lewis and Fannie's death soon after. "Babys are always dangerous but it is even more dangerous when you are old," she writes. "But everybody except me wants them, it is hard to see why" (9). Molly's ambivalence about Alice seems less derived from her motherhood and more from her fragile constitution; Alice was frail for much of Molly's life and depended on the care of the slaves who travelled with her from her South Carolina plantation home to Agate Hill. "Mamma loved gold jewelry but I am not a thing like Mamma," Molly asserts; "I am NOT. I like rocks instead" (12). Though she frequently quotes her mother and mines her vocabulary—"For ever and utterly gone, as Mamma used to say," she writes at one point—Molly's feelings about Alice are complex (20). She admires her mother's beauty and kindness but does not want to duplicate Alice's life. Molly's disconnect with her own mother and Fannie is reflected in her own devastating attempts to become a mother. After the death of her first child, Christabel, at age two, Molly loses five other babies, none of whom lives for more than three weeks. "I never once thought I would want a child," Molly tells BJ, Jacky's cousin, "but now I want it the worst in the world. . . . It is all I want" (296). Molly's desire to be a mother, and her subsequent reconciliation with the memory of her own mother, grow out of her biological and emotional maturation, and also from her belief that love and family are attainable for her.

It is not until Molly, aged and living again at Agate Hill, reads Simon Black's letter that she becomes reconciled to her memory of Alice. Molly reveals this peace when she writes in her diary about a new addition to her collection of relics. "It is a heart-shaped stirrup forged by Simon Black for my mother," she says; "I know all about it now" (333). Added to Molly's fine and expensive keepsakes of Alice—"the green liqueur glass from Venice, my mother's silver hairbrush"—the simple old stirrup represents an aspect of Alice's life that makes her a more relatable and sympathetic figure for Molly. Her mother was not simply a plantation princess surrounded by faithful devotees and luxury; she also was a feeling woman who was tempted to give it all up for Simon Black. Molly's enormous love for Jacky prepares her to understand Alice's choice. When she achieves a better understanding of Alice, Molly is finally allowed to be a mother herself by caring for Juney. Smith symbolizes this shift in Molly's role through the language that Juney uses to refer to his caretaker. "Over the years," Molly writes, "he has gone from calling me Molly, or something like Molly, to Ma, to Mamma, to Mammalee" (354). As Cook puts it, "Juney is the consolation of all the children Molly has buried, both daughter and son, child and adult" (Cook 220). Though finding Juney does not undo the pain of losing her biological children, he allows Molly to experience a sort of motherhood.

If Molly sometimes defines herself in opposition to other women, she is equally prone to aligning her subjectivity with that of other characters, some of whom are surprising. The earliest instance of this is Molly's friendship with

Mary White, her spunky but frail cousin visiting from Alabama. "The reason I have not written for so long Dear Diary," Molly writes after Mary White's arrival, "is that now I am a real girl with a real friend who . . . does everything with me" (43). Her friendship with Mary changes Molly's self-conception: she sees herself as "real" and even special instead of as an unlucky, lonely ghost when Mary White is with her. "Mary White knows all about fairies and now I do too," Molly writes, and she is excited that the fairies choose to appear to her and not to others (44). Though the girls' preoccupation with fairies may seem frivolous, it infuses Molly's previously grim life with a sense of magic, and the power of their supernatural visitations sustains Molly throughout her life. As Cook has written, fairies are representative of Molly's imagination, and the fact that Molly shares them with Mary White underscores the power of their bond. Molly writes to Mary White for most of her life, though she seldom receives replies and knows it is likely that her sickly friend has died. Like Ivy Rowe of *Fair and Tender Ladies* and her institutionalized sister Silvaney, Molly and Mary are entwined in one another's subjectivity; Mary is Molly's touchstone as well as her imaginative partner.

The more surprising of her intense identifications is Molly's relationship with Simon Black, who loved her mother and transfers that care to Molly. Initially Molly resents Simon's intrusions into her life. Because she does not understand why he follows and seeks to direct her, she rebuffs his efforts. When he comes to visit her at the Bobcat School, for instance, Molly's friend and colleague Agnes witnesses their heated conversation, after which Molly stamps her foot and tells Agnes that Black merely was "a stranger" who "had lost his way" (242). However, when Black purchases Agate Hill and Jacky has died, Molly finally feels ready to face her benefactor and her past. "*I have been waiting for this*," Molly writes when she sees him again. "It was the last thing left to happen to me" (328–29).

As Cook has written, Molly has been "mothered," whether or not she wanted to be, by Black for most of her life; after the loss of her own children and adult family, she returns to Agate Hill ready to mother him in kind. Black is ill when she arrives, and she throws herself into his care. "I stayed with him until his death," Molly writes, "flesh to flesh, bone to bone, pressing my body against . . . the whole long fragile length of him" (333). Though Molly does not explicitly explain what changed her feelings about Simon Black from resentment to intense understanding, the change itself is unmistakable. Upon his death she writes: "I lay beside him while all the changes took place, his ravaged body cooling, his thin arm growing stiff across my breast. We are like a sarcophagus, I thought. . . . Now we are the sarcophagus itself" (334). Even before she has read Simon's letter detailing his connection to Alice and his motivation for shadowing Molly, she feels eternally, supernaturally, bound to the man.

Molly's changed feelings about Simon Black and maternal figures in her early life hint at a larger evolution in her perspective that is evident upon her return to Agate Hill. The most profound expression of this shift is Molly's sense that, despite being absent for decades, she is the same essential self that she was when she left Agate Hill as a teenager. "I thought I would not know her anymore," Molly writes of her younger self, "and yet I find that I am her, just as wild and full of spite and longing as ever, as I still am" (332). She continues: "inside I am just the same and I'll swear it, still crazy with love and pain, still wanting who knows what." Molly feels differently about events and people in her young life, but she does not believe that shifts in her perspective constitute a significant change in who she is. What she does single out as different, though, are the middle years of her life, when she lived at Gatewood, Bobcat, and with Jacky. "I am not sure whatever happened to that smart girl in between, the one who kept the Bobcat School and worked at the store wrapping parcels and adding up sums in her head," she writes. "Oh Molly Petree, who were you?" (333). The novel suggests, by its arrangement, that it agrees with Molly; while most of Molly's time at Agate Hill is narrated in her own distinct voice, the sections in which she is away from the plantation largely are told through the voices of others. Thus it seems that Molly's journey away from and returning to Agate Hill has left her, in terms of her subjectivity, back where she started. What she has gained, emotionally and educationally, however, leaves her better able to live with the events of her and her family's pasts.

If there is a striking difference between the Molly Petree of 1872 and of 1927, it is in the terms she uses to define her own identity. Once she has grappled with her ghosts and assumed care of Juney, Molly conceives of herself in simple, practical terms rather than with the abstract language she chose as a child. The "ruby-throated hummingbird" and "ghost girl" have been replaced by a matter-of-fact role player. "I am the one who arranges the flowers," she writes, and "Henry is the one who will drive the car" (357). In the final section of the novel Molly frequently describes herself in terms of her actions, and nearly always includes the actions of her cobbled-together family members, Henry and Juney. "I am the one who arranges the flowers" she repeats in another diary entry. "I am the one who tells the stories, Henry is the one who drives the car" (359). Molly's feelings about what she must do are also noticeably more grounded. As a girl she worried about leaving behind the ghosts of her family's past if she left Agate Hill. As an older woman, though, Molly's concern is for the physical and emotional well-being of Juney, whom she cannot imagine leaving. While considering how important her care is for Juney, she writes, "So I can't die, for then who will do it? I think about this all the time" (353). Though the Molly of 1927 is still worried for others, this time she invests her worries in immediate concrete concerns. That she has not abandoned her imagination entirely, though, is suggested by her roles as storyteller and arranger of flowers.

Early in Molly's life she has an experience that is repeated at least three times in Smith's fiction. Lying in the frozen dark outside her home, Molly contemplates staying in the snow forever and thereby avoiding the worst parts of her hard life. But a fairy intrudes: "Wake up Molly Petree, he said in his high chirping voice. Go home. . . . I got up from the snow and hoisted my buckets and headed home" (105). Molly has more living to do, as did Ivy Rowe, who rouses herself from the snow in *Fair and Tender Ladies,* and Evalina Toussaint, who does the same in *Guests on Earth*. Evalina's version of this occurrence is Smith's most recent depiction. It reads: "I had nearly lost my life already, and now I wanted it. I wanted it all—that brass ring, the whole ball of wax. The world. I struggled desperately to get up. . . . The sky shone lighter now through the lacy black trees." *Morgen,* I remembered. *Morgen* (308).

Like Ivy and, in some ways, Evalina, Molly embodies the heart of Lee Smith's fiction. Beyond that, though, she is a manifestation of Smith's approach to writing and to life. In the *Dimestore* essay "Good-bye to the Sunset Man" Smith writes of her own struggle to get up out of the snow, as it were, after the death of her son. "To have children—or simply to experience great love for any person at all," she writes, "is to throw yourself open to the possibility of pain at any moment. But I would not choose otherwise. Not now, not ever" (135). Smith describes feeling free to die, now that her disabled child is gone. "But I don't want to," she says. "Instead, I want to live as hard as I can, burning up the days in honor of his sweet, hard life" (136). By creating characters like Molly, Smith does.

BIBLIOGRAPHY

Works by Lee Smith

BOOKS

Black Mountain Breakdown. New York: Ballantine, 1980.
Cakewalk. New York: Ballantine, 1981.
The Christmas Letters. Chapel Hill, N.C.: Algonquin Books, 1996.
Fair and Tender Ladies. New York: Ballantine, 1988.
Family Linen. New York: Ballantine, 1985.
Fancy Strut. New York: Ballantine, 1973.
The Devil's Dream. New York: Ballantine, 1992.
Dimestore. Chapel Hill, N.C.: Algonquin Books, 2016.
Guests on Earth. Chapel Hill, N.C.: Algonquin Books, 2013.
The Last Day the Dogbushes Bloomed. Baton Rouge: Louisiana State
    University Press, 1994
The Last Girls. Chapel Hill, N.C.: Algonquin Books, 2002.
Me and My Baby View the Eclipse. New York: Ballantine, 1990.
Mrs. Darcy and the Blue-Eyed Stranger. Chapel Hill, N.C.: Algonquin
    Books, 2010.
News of the Spirit. New York: Ballantine, 1997.
On Agate Hill. Chapel Hill, N.C.: Algonquin Books, 2006.
Oral History. New York: Ballantine, 1983.
Saving Grace. New York: Ballantine, 1995.
Sitting on the Courthouse Bench: An Oral History of Grundy, Virginia.
    Edited by Lee Smith. Chapel Hill, N.C.: Tryon Publishing, 2000.
Something in the Wind. New York: Harper & Row, 1971.

ESSAY

"In Her Words." *LeeSmith.com*, http://leesmith.com/guests_essay.pdf. Accessed May 5,
    2017.
"Showing Up for Work." *LeeSmith.com*, http://www.leesmith.com/works/showingup
    .php. Accessed September 17, 2012.

Selected Works about Lee Smith

INTERVIEWS

Ketchin, Susan. "Interview with Lee Smith." In *All Out of Faith: Southern Women on
    Spirituality*, edited by Wendy Reed and Jennifer Horne, 154–67. Tuscaloosa: Univer-
    sity of Alabama Press, 2006.

Tate, Linda, ed. *Conversations with Lee Smith*. Jackson: University Press of Mississippi, 2001.

"Waggoner, Martha. "Write Prescription for her Grief." *The Orange County Register*, http://www.ocregister.com/2007/01/21/write-prescription-for-her-grief/. Accessed 6 May 2017.

CRITICAL ANALYSES

Ammons, Jessie. "A Woman of Letters." *Chapel Hill Magazine*. July–August 2014, 66.

Barke, Megan, Rebecca Fribush, and Peter N. Stearns. "Nervous Breakdown in 20th-Century American Culture." *Journal of Social History* 33 (Spring 2000): 565–84.

Bauer, Margaret D. "Introduction: Crossing the Tracks of the Dixie Limited: Overcoming Anxiety of Influence and Filling in the Blanks." In *William Faulkner's Legacy*, 1–12. Gainesville: University Press of Florida, 2005.

———. "No Mere Endurance Here: The Prevailing Woman's Voice in Lee Smith's *Oral History*." *Pembroke Magazine*, Lee Smith Special Issue 33 (2001): 21–43.

Baym, Nina. "The Myth of the Myth of Southern Womanhood." In *Feminism and American Literary History: Essays*, 183–96. New Brunswick: Rutgers University Press, 1992.

Bennett, Tanya Long. "'It was like I was right there': Primary Experience and the Role of Memory in Lee Smith's *The Devil's Dream*." *Pembroke Magazine*, Lee Smith Special Issue 33 (2001): 86–92.

———. "The Protean Ivy in Lee Smith's *Fair and Tender Ladies*." *Southern Literary Journal* 30 (Spring 1998): 76–95.

Billips, Martha. "Siblings and Sex: A New Approach to the Fiction of Lee Smith." *Feminist Formations* 24 (Spring 2012): 127–53.

Burriss, Theresa L. "Claiming a Literary Space: The Affrilachian Poets." In *An American Vein: Critical Readings in Appalachian Literature*, edited by Danny L. Miller, Sharon Hatfield, and Gurney Norman, 315–36. Athens: Ohio University Press, 2005.

Butcher, Fanny. "Novels." *Chicago Tribune*, September 25, 1968.

Byrd, Linda. "The Emergence of the Sacred Sexual Mother in Lee Smith's *Oral History*." *Southern Literary Journal* 31 (Fall 1998): 119–142.

Campbell, H. H. "Lee Smith and the Brontë Sisters." *Southern Literary Journal* 33 (Fall 2000): 141–49.

Cavener, Jim. "On Agate Hill Lets Smith Shine in Solo Performance." *LeeSmith.com*, http://www.leesmith.com/works/batessmithreview.php. Accessed May 6, 2017.

Cook, Linda Byrd. *Dancing in the Flames: Spiritual Journey in the Novels of Lee Smith*. Jefferson, N.C.: McFarland, 2009.

Dale, Corrine. "The Power of Language in Lee Smith's *Oral History*." In *An American Vein: Critical Readings in Appalachian Literature*, edited by Danny L. Miller, Sharon Hatfield, and Gurney Norman, 184–96. Athens: Ohio University Press, 2005.

Donaldson, Susan V. "Telling Forgotten Stories of Slavery in the Postmodern South." *Southern Literary Journal* 40 (Spring 2008): 267–83.

Donlon, Jocelyn Hazelwood. "Hearing Is Believing: Southern Racial Communities and Strategies of Story-Listening in Gloria Naylor and Lee Smith." *Twentieth Century Literature* 41 (Spring 1995): 16–35.

Druesedow, Debra. "Place and Memory in Lee Smith's *Saving Grace*." *Pembroke Magazine*, Lee Smith Special Issue 33 (2001): 72–79.

Eckard, Paula Gallant. *Maternal Body and Voice in Toni Morrison, Bobbie Ann Mason, and Lee Smith.* Columbia: University of Missouri Press, 2002.

———. "The Prismatic Past in *Oral History* and *Mama Day*." *MELUS* 20 (Autumn 1995): 121–35.

Entzminger, Betina. *The Belle Gone Bad: White Southern Women Writers and the Dark Seductress.* Baton Rogue: Louisiana State University Press, 2002.

French, William W. "Review." *Theatre Journal* 40 (October 1988): 421–22.

Gebhard, Caroline "Reconstructing Southern Manhood: Race, Sentimentality, and Camp in the Plantation Myth." In *Haunted Bodies: Gender and Southern Text,* edited by Susan V. Donaldson and Anne Goodwyn Jones, 132–55. Charlottesville: University of Virginia Press, 1997.

Gilbert, Sandra M., and Susan Gubar. "Infection in the Sentence: The Woman Writer and the Anxiety of Authorship." In *Feminisms,* edited by Robyn R. Warhol and Diane Price Herndl, 21–32. New Brunswick: Rutgers University Press, 1997.

Gleeson-White, Sarah. "Revisiting the Southern Grotesque: Mikhail Bakhtin and the Case of Carson McCullers." *Southern Literary Journal* 33 (Spring 2001): 108–23.

Gussow, Mel. "Review/Theater: Spunky Southern Woman Tells All in a Monodrama." *NYTimes.com,* http://www.nytimes.com/1991/04/22/theater/review-theater-spunky-southern-woman-tells-all-in-a-monodrama.html. Accessed February 5, 2012.

Gwin, Minrose. "Introduction: Reading History, Memory, and Forgetting." *Southern Literary Journal* 40 (Spring 2008): 1–10.

———. "Nonfelicitous Space and Survivor Discourse: Reading Father-Daughter Incest." In *The Woman in the Red Dress: Gender, Space, and Reading,* 55–115. Chicago: University of Illinois Press, 2002.

———. "Space Travel: The Connective Politics of Feminist Reading." *Signs* 21 (Summer 1996): 870–905.

Hall, Joan Wylie. "Arriving Where She Started: Redemption at Scrabble Creek in Lee Smith's *Saving Grace*." *Pembroke Magazine,* Lee Smith Special Issue 33 (2001): 80–85.

Harington, Donald. "Lee Smith Mines the South's Rich Past." *The News and Observer* (Raleigh, NC), 17 October 2005, G5.

Helton, Tena. "Living in Process: Ivy Rowe's Regional Identification in *Fair and Tender Ladies*." *South Atlantic Review,* SAMLA Convention Issue, 69, no. 2 (2004): 1–24.

Hill, Dorothy Combs. *Lee Smith.* New York: Twayne, 1992.

Hirsch, Marianne. "Feminist Discourse/Maternal Discourse: Speaking with Two Voices." In *The Mother/Daughter Plot: Narrative, Psychoanalysis, Feminism,* 162–99. Indianapolis: Indiana University Press, 1989.

Hirsch, Marianne, and Valerie Smith. "Feminism and Cultural Memory: An Introduction." *Gender and Cultural Memory,* Special Issue, *Signs* 28 (Autumn 2002): 1–19.

Hobson, Fred. "Introduction." In *South to the Future: An American Region in the Twenty-First Century,* edited by Hobson, 1–12. Athens: University of Georgia Press, 2001.

Hoffman, Roy. "History's Child." *NYTimes.com,* http://www.nytimes.com/2006/10/08/books/review/Hoffman.t.html. Accessed September 18, 2012.

Homans, Margaret. "'Her Very Own Howl': The Ambiguities of Representation in Recent Women's Fiction." *Signs* 9 (Winter 1983): 186–205.

Hovis, George. *Vale of Humility: Plain Folk in Contemporary North Carolina Fiction.* Columbia: University of South Carolina Press, 2007.

Jones, Anne Goodwyn. "The World of Lee Smith." In *Women Writers of the Contemporary South*, edited by Peggy Whitman Prenshaw, 248–72. Jackson: University Press of Mississippi, 1984.

Jones, Suzanne W. "City Folks in Hoot Owl Holler: Narrative Strategy in Lee Smith's *Oral History*." *Southern Literary Journal* 20 (Fall 1987): 101–12.

Kalb, John D. "The Second 'Rape' of Crystal Spangler." *Southern Literary Journal* 21 (Fall 1988): 23–30.

Kearns, Katherine. "From Shadow to Substance: The Empowerment of the Artist Figure in Lee Smith's Fiction." In *Writing the Woman Artist: Essays on Poetics, Politics, and Portraiture*, edited by Suzanne W. Jones, 175–95. Philadelphia: University of Pennsylvania Press, 1991.

Kinsella, W. P. "Left Behind on Blue Star Mountain." *New York Times Book Review*, September 16, 1988, 9.

Lauter, Paul. "Caste, Class, and Canon." In *Feminisms*, edited by Robyn R. Warhol and Diane Price Herndl, 129–50. New Brunswick: Rutgers University Press, 1997.

"Lee's Brilliant Career." *NCSU Libraries*, http://www.lib.ncsu.edu/archivedexhibits/ smith/career.html. Accessed May 5, 2012.

Le Goff, Jacques. "Past/Present." In *History and Memory*, translated by Steven Rendall and Elizabeth Claman, 1–19. New York: Columbia University Press, 1992.

Lehmann-Haupt, Christopher. "Books of the Times." *NYTimes.com*, http://www .nytimes.com/1983/07/29/books/books-of-the-times-064790.html. Accessed June 5, 2017.

Locklear, Erica Abrams. *Negotiating a Perilous Empowerment: Appalachian Women's Literacies*. Athens: Ohio University Press, 2011.

Lowenthal, David. *The Past is a Foreign Country*. Cambridge: Cambridge University Press, 1985.

———. *Possessed By the Past: The Heritage Crusade and the Spoils of History*. Cambridge: Cambridge University Press, 1998.

MacKethan, Lucinda. "Artists and Beauticians: Balance in Lee Smith's Fiction." *Southern Literary Journal* 15 (Fall 1982): 3–14.

———. "'Multiple Personality Disorder': Speakers and Listeners in Lee Smith's Novels." *Blackbird: An Online Journal of Literature and the Arts*, http://www.blackbird.vcu .edu/v5n2/features/smith_l_12-20-06/review.htm. Accessed September 17, 2012.

McDonald, Jeanne. "Lee Smith at Home in Appalachia." In *Conversations with Lee Smith*, edited by Linda Tate, 178–88. Jackson: University Press of Mississippi, 2001.

McDowell, Robert W. "'Agate Hill to Appomattox,' A New One Woman Show by Barbara Bates Smith, Will Premiere at Deep Dish." *Triangle Arts & Entertainment*, http://triangleartsandentertainment.org/2012/06/agate-hill-to-appomattox-a-new -one-woman-show-by-barbara-bates-smith-will-premiere-at-deep-dish/. Accessed September 19, 2012.

Merser, Cheryl. "Lingering Letters of a 'Fair and Tender' Lady." *USA Today*, October 28, 1988, D5.

Miller, Danny L., Sharon Hatfield, and Gurney Norman, eds. *An American Vein: Critical Readings in Appalachian Literature*. Athens: Ohio University Press, 2005.

Ostwalt, Conrad. "Witches and Jesus: Lee Smith's Appalachian Religion." *Southern Literary Journal* 31 (Fall 1998): 98–118.

Parrish, Nancy C. *Lee Smith, Annie Dillard, and the Hollins Group: A Genesis of Writers*. Baton Rouge: Louisiana State University Press, 1998.

————. "Rescue from Oblivion: Letterwriting and Storytelling in Lee Smith's *Fair and Tender Ladies*." *Pembroke Magazine*, Lee Smith Special Issue 33 (2001): 114–21.

"Picks and Pans Review: Oral History." *People*, http://people.com/archive/picks-and -pans-review-oral-history-vol-20-no-5/. Accessed June 3, 2012.

Prajznerová, Katerina. *Cultural Intermarriage in Southern Appalachia: Cherokee Elements in Four Selected Novels by Lee Smith*. New York: Routledge, 2003.

Price, David W. "Introduction: Contending with History." In *History Made, History Imagined: Contemporary Literature, Poiesis, and the Past*, 1–18. Chicago: University of Illinois Press, 1999.

Ramos, Carmen Rueda. *Voicing the Self: Female Identity and Language in Lee Smith's Fiction*. Valencia, Spain: University of Valencia Press, 2009.

Reilly, Rosalind B. "*Oral History*: The Enchanted Circle of Narrative and Dream." *Southern Literary Journal* 23 (Fall 1990): 79–92.

Rifkind, Donna. "Educating Molly." washingtonpost.com, *Washington Post Book World*, October 1, 2006. Accessed September 17, 2012.

Robbins, Dorothy Dodge. "Personal and Cultural Transformation: Letter Writing in Lee Smith's *Fair and Tender Ladies*." *Critique* Winter 1997: 135–44.

Roberts, Diane. "Reconstruction Shapes Girl's Gothic Diary." *The Atlanta Journal-Constitution* (Atlanta, GA), September 17, 2006, L4.

Robinson, Lillian S. "Treason Our Text: Feminist Challenges to the Literary Canon." In *Feminisms*, edited by Robyn R. Warhol and Diane Price Herndl, 115–28. New Brunswick: Rutgers University Press, 1997.

Roth, Michael. "Remembering Forgetting." In *Memory, Trauma, and History: Essays on Living with the Past*, 3–22. New York: Columbia University Press, 2012.

Seidel, Kathryn Lee. *The Southern Belle in the American Novel*. Tampa: University of South Florida Press, 1985.

Skeggs, Beverley. "Ambivalent Femininities." In *The Body: A Reader*, edited by Mariam Fraser and Monica Greco, 129–34. New York: Routledge, 2005.

Smith, Rebecca. *Gender Dynamics in the Fiction of Lee Smith: Examining Language and Narrative Strategies*. San Francisco: International Scholars, 1997.

Tebbetts, Terrell. "Disinterring Daddy: *Family Linen*'s Reply to *As I Lay Dying*." *Southern Literary Journal* 38 (Spring 2006): 97–112.

Towers, Sarah. "Of Huck and Harriet." *NYTimes*.com, http://www.nytimes.com/2002/10/06/books/of-huck-and-harriet.html. Accessed September 10, 2013.

Town, Caren J. "'Becoming: Maybe So': Lee Smith." In *The New Southern Girl: Female Adolescence in the Works of 12 Women Authors*, 21–40. Jefferson, N.C.: McFarland, 2004.

Wagner-Martin, Linda. "'Just the Doing of It': Southern Women Writers and the Idea of Community." *Southern Literary Journal* 22 (Spring 1990): 19–32.

Wesley, Debbie. "A New Way of Looking at an Old Story: Lee Smith's Portrait of Female Creativity." *Southern Literary Journal* 30 (Fall 1997): 88–101.

Williamson, Joel. "Southern Genius in the Twentieth Century." In In *South to the Future: An American Region in the Twenty-First Century*, edited by Fred Hobson, 13–24. Athens: University of Georgia Press, 2001.

INDEX